Laymen Speaking

Laymen Speaking

selected and edited by
WALLACE C. SPEERS

ASSOCIATION PRESS
347 Madison Avenue, New York 17, N. Y.

1947

145

Foreword

THESE ARE THE WRITINGS OF LAYMEN who, having found something good and true and wonderful, feel some of the constraint of the Apostles of the early Church to share it with others. That discovery is, of course, the joyousness, the satisfaction, the necessity, and the workability of the Christian religion as a faith, a philosophy, and a pattern of personal living.

Dr. Fosdick has well expressed what they have come to feel: that the future of Christianity lies largely in the hands of laymen. Perhaps these talks do not offer the polished phrase of the skillful writer; they do offer an earnest and balanced conviction. These men are active participants in church affairs, and most of the talks collected here have been given on Laymen's Sunday and other church functions where laymen have assumed active leadership. *Laymen Speaking* is published in co-operation with the Laymen's Movement for a Christian World, which sponsors the annual observance of Laymen's Sunday.

Since its inception in 1941, the Laymen's Movement has endeavored to build a bridge between the religious life of the layman and his business affairs. For far too long, these have been considered as having no relation to each other. Once this bridge has been built in the minds of laymen, a Christian ap-

5

proach to community and world affairs becomes inescapable. That approach is clearly seen in these talks embracing religion in one's personal life, the layman's role in the Church, and the layman at work in the community and the world.

Men seem to work better toward the attainment of a generalized goal if provided with concrete tasks which, in the doing, yield a feeling of accomplishment and mutuality. One of these is Laymen's Sunday, held annually on the third Sunday of October. This service is conducted partially or entirely by laymen. Beginning in 1941 with 250 churches, the program spread until 1946 over 5,000 churches observed this day. Experience has shown that men who have taken part in these services have become more active in every department of the work of the churches and in community service.

In further efforts to induce men to apply religious principles to secular affairs, the Laymen's Movement has been conducting Labor-management Conferences and a Laymen's Call to Prayer in support of the United Nations. These conferences, with equal participation by labor and management, have demonstrated that there can be created an atmosphere in which both sides can rationally discuss their differences and better understand the problems of each. Because of our conviction that the United Nations can only succeed with an appreciation of the part that spiritual values play, the prayer call is an attempt to develop an increased awareness of the problems faced by the world's leaders and to help provide a sense of unity among people everywhere.

While *Laymen Speaking* cannot represent the point of view of all laymen, it is our prayerful hope that, in stimulating laymen and the clergy, it may help to close the gap between laymen and their ministerial leaders. Even more important, it may emphasize that laymen must participate actively and intelligently in local churches and in the affairs of the Church in general. The Church and the world need men who know as much about religion as they know about their jobs or local politics. From such an informed, practicing body of Christian laymen will emerge more alert lay leadership, giving new authority to church pronouncement, and new directions to politics, education, economics, social relations, and morals. This book indicates ways in which some laymen are taking the first steps forward.

For the Laymen's Movement
for a Christian World

WALLACE C. SPEERS
C. A. CAPRON
JOHN P. HOLMES
DAVID H. SCOTT

About These Laymen

EDMUND D. AYRES ("Wider Horizons Are Yours") is professor of electrical engineering at Ohio State University and is a member of Trinity Episcopal Church, Columbus, Ohio.

C. ALEXANDER CAPRON ("The God We Seek") is an attorney with Mitchell, Capron, March, Angulo and Cooney, and is a member of St. James Church (Protestant Episcopal) of Upper Montclair, New Jersey.

CHARLES J. CHANDLER ("World Security: A Personal Issue") is president of the First National Bank in Wichita, Kansas, and is a member of the Presbyterian Church.

JAMES S. CRUTCHFIELD ("Practical View of Labor Relations") is president of Union Fruit Auction Company and is a member of Sewickley, Pennsylvania, Presbyterian Church.

CHERRY L. EMERSON ("A New Scale of Values") is Dean of the School of Engineering, Georgia School of Technology, Atlanta, Georgia, and is a member of the Covenant Presbyterian Church.

MELVIN J. EVANS ("Bringing Life into Focus") is president of the Melvin J. Evans Company, Chicago, Illinois, and is a member of the Presbyterian Church.

9

EUGENE EXMAN ("Researchers of the Spirit") is manager of the Religious Book Department of Harper and Brothers and is a member of the Riverside Church, New York, New York.

WARFIELD M. FIROR ("Man's Dependence on God") is a surgeon at Johns Hopkins Hospital, Baltimore, Maryland, and is a member of the Franklin Street Presbyterian Church.

RALPH E. FLANDERS ("God's Law in Modern Life") is United States Senator from Vermont and is a member of the First Congregational Church, Springfield, Vermont.

LESTER B. GRANGER ("Tackling Negro-white Relationships") is executive secretary of National Urban League and is a member of St. Martins Episcopal Church, New York, New York.

W. H. GOODWIN ("Delivering the Goods") is a retired department store operator and is affiliated with the United Church of Canada.

JOHN P. HOLMES ("A Satisfied Customer") is vice-president of the Celanese Company and is a member of the Reformed Church of Bronxville, New York.

ARTHUR A. HOOD ("The Christian Economy") is vice-president of Vance Publishing Corporation, editor of American Lumberman and Building Products Merchandiser, and is a member of the Reformed Church of Bronxville, New York.

WEYMAN C. HUCKABEE ("How Men Respond to Religion") is secretary-treasurer of the Laymen's Movement for a Christian World and is a member of the Methodist Church.

MERRICK JACKSON ("Patterns of Christian Life in Business") is public-relations representative for Hill and Knowlton, New York, and is a member of the Baptist Church.

JAMES E. KAVANAGH ("The Church and Its Laymen") is recently retired from vice-presidency of Metropolitan Life Insurance Company and is a member of the Reformed Church of Bronxville, New York.

A. LUDLOW KRAMER ("A Businessman's Search for God") is a retired lawyer and banker, and is a member of the Presbyterian Church.

HAROLD S. MINER ("The Church and Our Responsibility") is vice-president of Manufacturer's Trust Company, New York, and is a member of Community Church, Great Neck, Long Island.

J. C. PENNEY ("Practice of Christian Principles") is the founder and honorary chairman of the board of the J. C. Penney Company, and is a member of the Community Church at Penney Farms, Florida.

JOHN J. PORTER ("Christianity Is Practical") is chairman of the board of the North American Cement Corporation and is a member of the St. Paul's Methodist Church in Hagerstown, Maryland.

JOHN G. RAMSAY ("Bridging the Gap") is representative of the Department of Public Relations, United Steelworkers of America, C.I.O.; community relations director, C.I.O. Organizing Committee; and is a member of the Presbyterian Church, U.S.A.

JOHN D. ROCKEFELLER, JR. ("God Is Man's Crying Need") has devoted the greater part of his life to the business, philanthropic, charitable, and civic undertakings of the Rockefeller family. He is a member of the Riverside Church, New York, and of its Board of Trustees.

FREDERICK C. SHIPLEY ("Christianity Outside the Church") is assistant professor of English and director of the Summer Session at the City College of New York, and is a member of the South Presbyterian Church, Dobbs Ferry, New York.

WALLACE C. SPEERS ("A Workable Human Society") is vice-president of James McCutcheon and Company and is a member of the Central Presbyterian Church in Montclair, New Jersey.

THOMAS J. WATSON ("Trends in America Affecting Our Economic Life") is president of International Business Machines Corporation and is a member of the Brick Presbyterian Church, New York, New York.

Contents

V. *The Layman at Work in the World*

Introduction

HARRY EMERSON FOSDICK

GOD CALLS MEN TO BE MINISTERS—yes, but just as truly God calls men and women to Christian laymenship. Statistics of church membership notoriously misrepresent the Church's real spiritual power. About half the population of the United States are Christian lay folk, but that is counting noses, not gauging spiritual strength. Millions of Christian lay folk have only this much relationship with God— they believe that there is a God, and once in a while they turn to him for help. That is about the sum of it. But turn now to the Bible and from one end to the other one finds another kind of experience altogether—men confronting God, running headlong into him, stopped in their tracks with a call, a commission, a sense of vocation from which in vain they try to flee. From Moses at the burning bush, taking the shoes from off his feet because the place whereon he stands is holy ground and receiving a commission he cannot escape, or Isaiah in the Temple, hearing a voice divine that he cannot refuse: "Whom shall I send, and who will go for us?" and answering, "Here am I; send me"; to Peter, James, and John, summoned by Christ to follow him, or Paul stopped dead on the Damascus Road with a challenge that transforms his life—such experience, the divine-human encounter from which one goes out under orders

17

with a great vocation, is the very heart of the Bible's religion.

Each of these typical men I have just named was a layman. None was a priest, an official ecclesiastic.

Consider, for one thing, that Christian laymen confront, as Isaiah did, a call of God in the social tragedy of our time. Isaiah's vocation in the Temple was intimately personal, but the background of it was international disaster. "Your country is desolate," Isaiah cried, "your cities are burned with fire; your land, strangers devour it in your presence, and it is desolate."

Well, the times are evil. Today God stands, as it were, with his hand on mankind's shoulder, saying: You are going through to a world organized for peace. You've got to! But man says, I will not; I want peace, but I will not pay the price. I will have my wars, my racial prejudice, my hatreds, my national sovereignties intact. Nevertheless, says God, you have come a long way since I started with you. And you are coming now, farther, much farther, than you have ever dreamed, or else—or else!

Such a situation does constitute a personal call to all of us. To the ministry; yes. But see! the areas where this new age must win its victories are where laymen live—politics, business and finance, racial relationships, the great professions, community service, the Church itself, where ministers come and go, but where the abiding continuum is the great body of the laymen. God needs the right kind of laymen, not merely believing in God and occasionally seeking his help, but confronting him and his call and accepting his commission.

If we could have our churches filled with lives in whom Christ had come through that far, we could move the world. Today, after long years in the ministry, I am thinking of the loyal laymen and laywomen with whom it has been my privilege to work. They carried Christ where I could never go; they exhibited the Christian spirit in relationships I never had a chance at; they wrought reforms in their businesses and professions that were utterly beyond my reach; they served the community in ways that no minister can compass, and put their intelligence and skill at the disposal of the Church, with results that I never dreamed were possible. Don't tell me that men and women are not called of God to Christian laymanship.

In the old days, there was a leper colony in Massachusetts that was later moved to an island in Buzzards Bay. The state could find no one to take care of them, and so Dr. Parker, who had served them on the mainland, gave up his practice in Plymouth and went out to live for fifteen years with the lepers on their island. One day a dying sailor asked for a Roman Catholic priest and Parker went to the mainland and got one. Sitting down beside the dying man, the priest asked, "Do you believe in God?" and the sailor answered, "I don't know whether I believe in God or not, but I believe in Dr. Parker." I suspect the priest accepted that. After all, that is the only place where a lot of people are going to see and recognize God—in the Dr. Parkers, the laymen and laywomen who meet them in the everyday relationships of life. It is not sacrilegious to believe in God in Dr. Parker. Do we not believe in God in Christ? Have

not all of us at some time, shaken by the vast mystery
of this universe, said: I don't know what I think
about God, but I believe in Christ. Well, Christ was
a layman.

Now come to the practical nub of this matter, as
it applies to our churches. The identification of the
church with the minister, as though the church were
to be thought of in terms of the preacher's name, as
a play on Broadway is associated with its star per-
former, is its major weakness. Ministers come and
go, they serve their day in one parish and move on
to another, or they grow old and pass off the scene;
but the permanent, ongoing stream of the Christian
fellowship is the lay body.

The continuous growth of the Church ushers in
the great mass of laymen who really believe in the
Church, and I should think that many lax, half-
hearted lay folk would be stirred today to a new and
moving faith in her. Granted, all the Church's
faults! They are often disheartening. But these are
troubled days when we must make the most of every
saving, hopeful factor in mankind's life, and the
Church of Christ is high on that list.

Our hope now lies in men and women in whose
eyes Christ and the heritage he stands for, and the
continuing fellowship that must conserve and further it, are paramount. We thank God today for men
and women who have answered that call.

I

The Personal and Social Need for Religion

A Workable Human Society

WALLACE E. SPEERS

I WOULD LIKE TO EMPHASIZE the critically important role of religion if we are to have a world of the future of the kind we all want.

We are in a world where we have nearly everything — power, wealth, production ability, skilled labor, efficient management, scientific knowledge, even genius. The main thing that is missing is the spirit that will make it all work. That spirit comes from religion, for it stems from the love of God and a desire to do his will. I do not say that in a sentimental or emotional manner, but rather in a cold, hard, realistic way.

There is a pattern of workability for the world contained in the laws of God for human conduct. If one will examine the perfectly functioning system of nature he will discover that all inanimate objects obey implicitly the laws of God. Crystal structures always break up in the same form; chemical elements always unite in the same proportions; the sun, moon, and stars travel around in prescribed orbits and on a definite time schedule.

Mankind, on the other hand, has been given the freedom of intelligent choice. There are laws of God for human conduct which replace the fixed laws for inanimate objects, but mankind does have the right to choose whether he will obey them or not.

It is an awe-inspiring choice, for upon whether the decision is to obey or not to obey rests the entire workability of the world. Indeed, the laws of God for human conduct are the laws of workability in mankind's use of things.

One does not break the laws of God; one merely disobeys them. One does not break the law of gravity by jumping out of a window. He merely disobeys it and gets punished by being badly hurt. One does not break the laws of God for human conduct; one merely disobeys them and gets punished by having a world that doesn't work.

I arrived at the conviction through the back door. In spite of a very religious upbringing, I did not attend church for many years. But, as a result of studying the conditions in Europe on business trips which I made once or twice a year between the two wars, as well as the conditions in this country, I was forced to the conclusion that if one is intellectually honest and knows the facts, the solution of any problem in human affairs is inescapably and inevitably in the principles of religion and the laws of God for human conduct.

A year ago I made a trip to Europe on the *Queen Mary*. I had a letter of introduction to a professor of political economy in Cambridge, England, who is also one of the editors of the *Manchester Guardian*. I met him one day on deck and remarked upon how terrible he looked, and asked him if he was sick. He said no, but that he had been up all night with a group of men in someone's cabin discussing world affairs. The group of men turned out to be the head of another government, an air-chief marshal, a famous war correspondent and author, a radio news analyst, an attorney-general, and himself. He said they had been discussing the whole night long the conditions in the various countries in the world, looking for some pinpoint of hope, and they found none. Finally, about 4 A.M., one of the men present summed up the discussion by saying, "There is every evidence to indicate that this is the end of the world, and that mankind is the composite devil who is going to destroy himself."

I said that I would agree with him that there is every evidence to indicate that this is so, but that over against this is the greatest potential for human benefit that ever existed in the history of the world, if we could get human relations fixed up. This was easy to say and hard to do, for it was the thing that the human race has been trying to accomplish since the dawn of civilization. Then I expressed to him my conviction that there is a pattern of workability for the world contained in the laws of God for human conduct.

He said, "I will agree with you to this extent. The atomic bomb and other disintegrating factors in the world's life have brought about a situation where any argument about what you are going to do and what you are going to let anyone else do is completely hypothetical and academic, for unless you do what your conscience tells you is right, and unless you help everyone to live and live adequately, you are just not going to be here. The ultimate in selfishness is to be completely unselfish.

"For the time being, this situation has the world's leaders completely lost, for they are up against the actual necessity of having to sell to a group of hard-boiled politicians and statesmen a bill of goods that sounds like nothing but 'sweetness and light' and they do not know where to start, or how."

I replied, "You are saying exactly what I said, that there is a pattern of workability for the world contained in the laws of God for human conduct."

He said, "I do not know as much about religion as you seem to, but I will quote the Scripture right back at you: 'This is the acceptable year of our Lord.' For God's sake, and I say it reverently, for God's sake, my dear sir, if what you say is true, you'd better get going with it!"

That statement sticks in one's mind and sets one on fire with the burning urgency of getting men everywhere to study and apply the laws of God to the affairs of everyday life, and to do it right now.

The American people have a particular flare, amounting almost to genius, for finding out how things work and then making them work. An airforce general made the statement that we would win the war because the American boy was born with a screwdriver and a chisel in his hand instead of a gun. Our men knew how to make machinery work. When we have a new car, or an icebox, or a piece of machinery of any kind that has a list of instructions with it, we are very apt to read these instructions and follow them out to the letter.

With that in mind, I would like to state a very simple proposition: We want a better world. The good Lord made the world and told us how it could be made to operate successfully. He said that the successful operation of the world was based entirely on his two commands, "Love the Lord thy God with all thy heart, with all thy mind and with all thy strength"; and, "Love thy neighbor as thyself." The first is the spiritual conditioning, or intake side, and the second is the practical, or distribution side, and we must maintain a complete balance between the two. If all of our time is spent on the spiritual intake side it becomes so comfortable and spiritually self-satisfying that it is apt to be completely paralyzing as far as practical effort is concerned. If all of our time is spent on the practical side, it is no doubt good, but it lays one open to all the errors to which human beings are prone.

The statement was made some time ago that the practice of the Golden Rule without imagination is irritation. We are apt to treat other people as we would like to treat them, rather than to treat them as we would like to be treated, and it just makes them angry. To reach our maximum effectiveness we must work as hard as we can and condition that effort by the use of spiritual values. Even expert ability becomes more adequate in the service of mankind when we keep in contact with God. One finds the necessity for maintaining this balance all through the affairs of everyday life.

I believe, for instance, that mass production is not permanently possible without mass distribution, and adequate mass distribution is impossible to achieve without the realization of the part that spiritual values play in everyday life. We are in an industrial age from which we cannot withdraw, whether we want to or not. Yet the very mass production upon which that age is built has a ceiling upon its possibilities for permanent success and continual progress which is in direct ratio to our appreciation and use of a sense of duty, justice, brotherhood, and the Golden Rule.

One can divide the income of a firm between management, labor, suppliers of raw material, stockholders, and all the other factors that enter into it, and it will be good arithmetic; it may be good cost accounting, but it does not become economics that will fit into a total economic picture, that will avoid strikes, depressions, and war, until one applies spiritual values to this division and changes it accordingly.

From the other side of the picture, it is equally true. Unless, and until, these same spiritual values are applied to the cause of industrial strife, any artificial stoppage of production is an uneconomic act which will cause as much harm to the well-being of labor as to management and the public.

We are entering an age of distribution. One can muddle through an age of production, but an age of distribution simply will not work as a matter of economics alone, unless the spiritual values are applied to the operations of industry and commerce.

This is also true in government. We can have the finest structure of government that the mind of man can conceive, but unless we have a population at work within that structure that is thoroughly imbued with the part that spiritual values play in everyday life, we do not have much of anything. Particularly we do not have democracy or freedom. Democracy is nothing but an attempt to apply the principles in the Bible to human society.

Our forefathers came together in a common faith in one God. They printed it on their money, "In God We Trust." Then they said to one another, "Under this faith we do not need a king, or dictator, or an over-all ruler, because we respect one another and we value one another's individuality, personality, and freedom. Furthermore, we are determined that the rights of each individual to life, liberty, and the pursuit of happiness, are the responsibility of all individuals to maintain and further." In so far as we have lost this concept of democracy, in just so far have we lost the beating heart that would set men on fire with the conviction that the good Lord meant the soul of man to be gloriously free. Eternal vigilance may be the price of freedom, but mutual responsibility is the coin with which the bill must be paid.

Take the present industrial situation as an example. A great many people think that our enormous and complex industrial enterprise is the product of smartness and superior knowledge. No doubt a great deal of this went into creating it. However, its successful operation is entirely dependent on the interdependence of man, and when that breaks down it goes to pieces.

Democracy is an equilibrium between wealth development and education balanced on spiritual values. When the spiritual values decrease, it goes inevitably to statism or communism. When the spiritual values increase, it goes just as inevitably toward the perfection of democracy. Communism cannot be licked by being afraid of it, or by being mad at it. It can only be licked by having a better answer. That

answer is in the principles of religion expressed in
very real terms of the opportunity to earn adequate
food, clothing, and shelter. Communism may have
wealth development and education and other things.
The one thing it cannot have is spiritual values, because as soon as it does it starts to develop toward democracy. Communism is not people. It is a condition.
It comes upon a democracy, not because some dynamic group tries to superimpose it. It will come, if
it ever does, because ordinary folks have not applied
the spiritual values of sense of duty, justice, human
understanding, and mutual responsibility to the
operations of industry and commerce, without being
forced to do so by government or the demands of
labor unions, but because there is something burning inside them that makes them love God and
fellow man.

In other words, the good Lord is telling us that
if we want a world that will work externally, we must
be responsible for the well-being of all people everywhere or we shall run into the possibility of attack
by "have-not" nations. And internally we must be
responsible for the well-being of all citizens in our
society or we lay ourselves open to the infiltration of
communism.

The good Lord told us how the world could be
made to work successfully. He said it was built on
love. Love is not silly sentimentalism or emotional-
ism, but is mutual respect, mutual understanding,
mutual faith, and mutual responsibility.

Upon these non-physical aspects of love rests the
entire ability of the human race to progress.

In other words, the world is crying for a spiritual

revival, not in the ordinary evangelistic terms, but in terms of what people have to live and work with every day of their lives. If that is so, what can we do about it? We can, all of us, make a thorough study of our business and try to align it according to the findings developed from our attempt to apply spiritual values to its operation.

Even more important, we can attempt to make use of the conditioning power of religion. That is a force that some of us have discovered works with great effectiveness, and in a very practical way. We have found in industrial relations conferences, which have been set up frankly on the basis of research projects into religion as an industrial method, that there is an atmosphere that can be created by spiritual conditioning, in which men can sit down together, no matter what side they are on, as friends, and think and talk and plan constructively for the mutual benefit of all concerned. That means prayer. Prayer is the single most powerful force in the world today.

When I went off in the first World War, my mother said to me, "Wallace, just because you have not been a good Church member does not mean that you cannot pray to God when you are scared." Being scared most of the time, I am afraid that I bothered the good Lord a good deal. As a result, I formed the habit of making a quiet little prayer whenever things were bigger than I was—which has been a good part of the time.

It is that kind of persistent personal prayer that I recommend that all men use. Let it be tried on the hardest people, not for the purpose of pushing them down, but that God's spirit of workability should surround them, and that they should feel God's love gently pushing them toward solutions to their problems benefiting all mankind. No one need know when prayer is being practiced in that way.

There is a pattern of workability for the world contained in the laws of God for human conduct. It is about time that we get going with it.

Man's Dependence on God

WARFIELD M. FIROR

ALMIGHTY and most merciful Father, we have erred, and strayed from thy ways like lost sheep. We have followed too much the devices and desires of our own hearts. We have offended against thy holy laws. We have left undone those things which we ought to have done; and we have done those things which we ought not to have done; And there is no health in us. But thou, O Lord, have mercy upon us, miserable offenders. Spare thou them, O God, which confess their faults. Restore thou them that are penitent; according to thy promises declared unto mankind In Christ Jesus our Lord. And grant, O most merciful Father, for his sake, that we may hereafter live a godly, righteous, and sober life, to the glory of thy holy Name. *Amen.*

There are various ways by which human beings can enter into communion with God. One of them is through the medium of music; another is by silence; and still another is by the medium of words. This, of course, is the most used. When we study the authoritative word of God, we are using that medium. Usually when we pray, we use it. Let us direct our thoughts to some words with which all of us are familiar—so familiar that sometimes they become trite. I refer to what is known as the General Confession.

This body of words is more than 300 years old, and it begins with this arresting phrase: "Almighty and most merciful Father." To the heathen. the idea of God's omnipotence was not strange. They were aware of his unlimited power and this evoked in them a sense of fear. They felt that they had to appease God; and all sorts of offerings, sacrifices and rituals were devised to thwart the untoward demonstrations of God's power, culminating, of course, in the sacrifice of one's child to appease the Deity.

The Christian concept of God's omnipotence is not based primarily upon a demonstration of physical energy but upon the idea that God has shown his omnipotence in creating a race of beings who are endowed with a very dangerous power, namely, the power of freedom, the ability to say No or Yes to God Almighty. That is a demonstration of much greater power than mere physical energy because the latter is great only by comparison. God is Almighty because he has given us the capacity of saying Yes or No, of being free to vote ourselves into his family or out of it.

The second phrase: "Most merciful Father." No other religion ever seriously considered God as a father until Christianity was revealed. Any father knows what is connoted in that term, how much is really desired for a son, how anxious he is for him to accept his standards, be responsive to his teaching and instruction, to profit by his mistakes, and to excel him! But, above all, the thing that every father wants most is a thoroughgoing reciprocal understanding between his son and himself. Then when one adds the adjective, "most merciful," and stops to think that the mercy is as great as the power, one inevitably feels one's own inadequacy. "Almighty and most merciful Father, Creator of the Universe," whose attitude toward me is that of mine toward my child, inevitably makes one feel his own inadequacy.

"We have erred and strayed from thy ways like lost sheep." Anyone who has lived on a farm knows that sheep have certain characteristics. One is that they follow a leader. A second is that they are easily frightened. A third is that they are stupid; they can't possibly find their way home. A dog, a cat, a horse, a cow, any domestic animal has more wisdom and sense than a sheep. So we, too, have strayed from God's eternal spiritual kingdom; we are easily frightened; we blindly follow after strange leaders; we do not know how, with our own efforts, to find the way home. We are like sheep. We have followed too much the devices and the desires of our own hearts. We have tried our own schemes. We have used our own logic. We have substituted our own desires. We have given first place to security, thinking that if we have security we can then be preoccupied with the kingdom of God.

"We have offended against thy holy laws." The law of Moses directed man's action. It told what one should do and should not do. Overt acts were the subject of that body of law. The Sermon on the Mount goes to the motives and purposes that prompt the acts. Whenever one hears a person say he "lives the Sermon on the Mount," think twice, because the

Sermon on the Mount is the most penetrating body
of law that we have ever inherited. It goes right
down to the heart of a man's intentions. The law
was given to show how absolutely impossible it is
for us to keep it.

"We have left undone those things which we
ought to have done, and we have done those things
which we ought not to have done. There is no
health in us." What is meant by the word "health"?
Well, it might be defined as that state in which all of
one's functions are working in harmony. They are
integrated into a unit and any deviation constitutes
sickness. If one looks a little more carefully into the
concept of health, he realizes that there are a great
number of control mechanisms that are working all
the time to maintain that harmony. Let me give you
a simple example: If we take the temperature of
everyone in New York City tonight who is well, there
will be a deviation of less than one degree centigrade.
The control mechanism is working. If we go up to
Alaska or down to the Equator and take the temperature of people there, it will be the same as it is in
New York. A control mechanism is at work night
and day that keeps our body temperature constant.

I mention the fact to point out that this phrase,
"there is no health in us," means that there is no
source of spontaneous control for our spiritual lives.
We are not endowed with a mechanism whereby,
when we stray from God's purpose, we automatically
swing back into it. We have control mechanisms to
maintain our physical well-being but not our spiritual. There is no source of health within us.

"But thou, O Lord, have mercy upon us miserable

offenders." Recently I think those last two words have been deleted. It is quite all right to delete them, if one would substitute more accurate adjectives. If one compares oneself to the Creator of the Universe and thinks of the wisdom, the generosity, the light, the energy, the goodness, the patience, the mercy of God, he will realize that the term "miserable offender" is inadequate. We really are diseased, disintegrated, worthless, indifferent, irresponsive, wayward children who have absolutely no merit in ourselves. We are disoriented; we have lost our bearing; our spirtual awareness is atrophied.

"Spare them, O God, which confess their faults." We are worthy of nothing but punishment. After all, how have we lived? We have squandered our opportunity; we have been preoccupied with material possessions. We have been spiritually sick.

"Spare thou them, O God, which confess their faults. Restore thou them that are penitent." The genius of Christianity lies in the fact that it demonstrates renewal. We have the capacity of being restored, renewed. There is no other teaching in the world which is so full of that concept of renewal. The Mosaic law said a person should forgive his brother seven times if he turned around and said, "I'm sorry," and Jesus said, "seventy times seven." That is his idea of God's attitude toward us—renewal.

"Restore thou them that are penitent." That word "penitent" bears some scrutiny. It is not remorse, though frequently mistaken for it. Remorse is the scrutiny of one's errors without hope. One has taken the wrong turn on the road, has gone far into an un-

known part of the country, has missed connections
and his friends, does not know where he is. It is
too late to do anything else; the whole journey is a
failure and he despairs of being able to do anything
about his mistakes. That's remorse—the scrutiny of
one's mistakes without hope—whereas penitence, or
repentance, is the scrutiny of those same mistakes
with hope. There is still time to turn around, correct one's way, get back on the highway, make
connections.

Renewal, then, is an essential part of Christianity,
and the amazing thing is that time doesn't enter into
God's computation. The thief on the cross had only
a few minutes to live, but he had repentance, renewal.

"Restore thou them that are penitent; according
to thy promises declared unto mankind in Christ
Jesus our Lord." One would like to enumerate some
of those promises, but let it suffice to give just one:
"No man knoweth the Father but the Son, and no
man knoweth the Son but the Father, and he to
whom he will reveal him." And then in the very
next sentence, "Come unto me, all ye who are weary
and heavy laden. I will give you rest."

"And grant, O merciful Father, for his sake, that
we may hereafter live"—not talk about it, not profess
it, live it—"that we may hereafter live a godly,
righteous, and sober life." We may live his life. We
have the capacity of being integrated with the most
merciful heavenly Father. We have the capacity of
being one with him. Take the seventeenth chapter
of John. The great burden of the prayer that Jesus

made for us was that we would be one with him as he was one with the Father.

Read the last seven or eight verses of the seventeenth chapter of John and realize what a stupendous privilege we have that we might live a godly life —just as if Jesus Christ permeated our lives. When we walk down the street, he walks down the street. We make a decision, it is Christ making the decision. That is exactly what he wants us to attain — a righteous life, one with his standards of values, "to the glory of thy holy name."

I have said before, and it bears repetition, that the essential meaning of the word "glory" is to give adequate expression to the true nature of something. When it is said, "Man's chief aim is to glorify God," one can translate that as: "Man's chief aim is to give adequate expression to God's real nature." This common or General Confession closes then with this petition: "Grant, O most merciful Father, for his sake, that we may hereafter live a Godly, righteous, and sober life, to give adequate expression to thy real nature."

Researchers of the Spirit

Eugene Exman

ONE OF THE MOST SATISFYING EXPERIENCES given
to man is to know that life has meaning. It is
good to meditate on the fact that ours is not a ca-
pricious, unpredictable world, but one of design and
dependability. This we know from our own limited
observations of cause and effect and from the reports
brought back by the scientists whose furthest steps
into the unknown are upheld by law and order. Prescribed regulations bring predictable results.

Today's paradox, however, is that this knowledge
brings, not satisfaction, but perplexity. We are beset
by a deep uneasiness. We know that Mr. Einstein's
formula $(E = MC^2)$ works and may some time work
so well that there will be no one left even to write
a note of sympathy and regret. Obviously this fear
and distress is not because of the formula but because
of ourselves. We have gone clear through graduate
school to learn how law operates in the world of
nature, but we are no further than the third grade
in studying the operation of law in the world of man.
Recently Dr. Edwin McNeill Poteat has urged scientists to conduct research in the laws of individual
and social living, which we can be taught to obey as
respectfully as the laws of the laboratory are obeyed.
The preacher asks the layman to look for moral law
and chart its cause and effect.

This is a valid challenge and merits consideration. It is directed, however, not to the skilled technician alone, but to all intelligent adults—truckdrivers, professors, housewives, coalminers, lawyers, publishers, farmers, doctors, mechanics, poets. Each of us has his laboratory of daily living in which he can work, if he wills to do so, with the same skill and persistence as at Oak Ridge.

But, you say, haven't we got the Bible to tell us right and wrong? And aren't the principles of Christianity pretty generally agreed upon? Moreover, the United Nations is man's new venture destined to bring peace and happiness to humanity at last. Can't we trust the Church and the statesmen to show us what needs doing?

These are good questions. Unhappily we can't be sure after nineteen centuries whether the Sermon on the Mount can or should be taken seriously. Claims of Catholics are met by counterclaims of Protestants. Each group is divided horizontally into parties or sects that often speak bitterly of the others. Each is divided vertically into theological or creedal groups —fundamentalist, sacramentalist, liberal, liturgist, neo-orthodox, humanist. Where, in organized religion, may unity, harmony, or unbiased leadership be found? And if churchmen can't agree, is there any likelihood that statesmen can settle their differences amicably? The United Nations will certainly not succeed so long as suspicion outruns trust.

Moreover, the churches and the nations are made up of groups of individuals. As individuals are, so the groups become; as individual persons we share responsibility for the future. Maybe the only hope is that we attempt to discover for our day what the laws are that govern human conduct. It is a life and death matter. I suggest that our venture, our research, should be directed to a new understanding of God, of our fellows and of ourselves.

All scientific researchers work from a hypothesis. Let our hypothesis be that this is a dependable universe created and sustained by a Power we call God, with a corollary that no event, no act, and no incident occurs without this event or act or incident being within God's knowledge and under God's control.

If this hypothesis be true—and most persons would likely assent to it—then it follows that man's chief concern should be to obtain as much knowledge and experience of God as it is possible to get. For a trout fisherman, knowledge about the nature and habits of trout, of the streams where trout may be found, of the best equipment and how it is used are essential if he is to enjoy his days of fishing. So it is with every vocation and every avocation. The greater a man's study and mastery of his calling, the greater his success is likely to be. If we would achieve mastery in this most important of all pursuits, the study of what and where God is and how he works, then we must give the best of our time and talents to the work.

But, one says, it isn't easy to learn about God. Does not one, first of all, need to have a great desire to be a fisherman before giving time and money to the pursuit? And does not one need to have a clearly defined field of study—not the whole universe? To both questions the obvious answer is, Yes. In the first place, no one will search after God unless he has an inner urge, unless he is more than casually a religious man. A grace of God is what the theologians term this inner drive that knows no rest till it rests in God. In the second place, a clearly defined area of study and work does need to be laid out. This is why we have churches, and, in my opinion, the degree to which a church can be said to be doing its job is determined by how well and consistently it gives direction and help to its people in this search after God.

At this point someone is sure to say that such talk as this is "escapism," so it may well be to repeat the hypothesis that the most important fact in life is that creative and sustaining unity which we call God, and the most neglected task is the study of man's relation to God. Certainly the work of the so-called "realists," who scoff at such a proposal as this, has not been noticeably successful. Man's preoccupation with man seems now to lead only to fear and futility— perhaps ultimately to world chaos and complete despair. Furthermore, it is just possible that the more we know about God the more we will know about man.

This leads to my second point—that we need to carry on research to find a new understanding of our fellows. This second understanding follows naturally from the first. No man can come into the knowledge of God without seeing his brother in a new light. Restitution follows conversion as surely as Monday follows Sunday. Charity toward others is a natural fruit of the life lived close to God. We see our fellows as those who also work or should work as we now venture to do. We believe that the design of God as evidenced in the outer universe is evidenced also in the existence of one another. Look at your relatives, your friends, your strangers met in passing as those who too are here not just for fun, fame, or fortune but to be found of God. You will see them in a new light.

To see our fellows in a new light is to treat them in a new way. This gets us into the field of ethics, and the key word from the New Testament is *agape,* "love." Unhappily, this word has been spoiled for many because it is generally used in a sentimental or pious way. We need to remind ourselves that love is not to be considered a matter of the emotions but an act of the will. Research here is greatly needed. How can we hold positive good will for all persons we deal with? Loud and influential voices (surprisingly, among them are some of the religious leaders of our day) cry out that it can't be done. We are, they say, living in a world of constant flux with new situations calling for new moral concepts. Tomorrow's action is predicated on today's tension between relative good and relative evil. They deride us as "perfectionists," and this epithet comes alongside that of "escapists" to distract and discourage those who would do research in living, under God, on terms of compassion for all creatures at all times. True, it is a difficult undertaking to strive for so high a goal and the prospect would be dismal indeed were it not for the assurance that God also works and that "all things are possible to him that believeth."

This compassionate understanding leads inevitably to companionship. We become co-workers with those who share our concern. Salvation is not a private matter. We need others as others need us. The spiritual renewal which brings men together in love of God and of their fellows is what periodically revives an established church or starts a new one. This work with a group for prayer, reading, and discussion points a way ahead. Without doubt the laboratories in which significant research in ethics will be carried on in the immediate future will be these hundreds of "cell" groups in towns, villages, and cities throughout the land.

Finally, our research into the laws that determine our existence should carry us to some important discoveries about ourselves. Who am I? One hypothesis is: A child of God in this phenomenal world of things and activity, a world apparently suited to and welcoming our work. The Archbishop of Canterbury was recently comparing the first question in the catechism of the Scottish Church to that of the Church of England, pointing out that his clerical friends in Scotland always ask, "What is the chief end of man?" while the more matter-of-fact Englishman queries, "What is your name?"

Whether we are of a metaphysical or practical mind, we do surely face this second question, What am I to do? Again, one hypothesis on which researchers will be working is: A man's job is to grow a soul, a continuum of experience that begins here and extends beyond. How this is done these researchers will be telling us, though the saints and mystics, more respected in other times than in our own, have blazed the trail. They urge us to work with increasing intelligence and vigor to rid ourselves of greed and covetousness, to become less at-

tached to things and events—even persons—as ends
in themselves. A sense of humor helps, for man's
common tendency, ever since Lucifer, to take himself too seriously is not easily sloughed off. They
also insist that we must save time out of each day to
follow the discipline of prayer. If by training we can
become pure in heart — of pure intent — then the
promise is that we may see God. But we must be
practised in knowing where and how to look. Regu-
larity of times of prayer, reading in carefully selected
books, and frequent recollection during the ordinary
events of every day—these are elementary prerequi-
sites. At the same time, our work and our friends
give us help and the triangle of God, others, and
self is made complete.

> Grow old along with me!
> The best is yet to be
> The last of life, for which the
>   first was made.

God's Law in Modern Life

RALPH E. FLANDERS

WHEN WE LOOK BACK over the last two hundred years, we realize that human life in this world has changed beyond all recognition, so far as its material aspects are concerned. This has resulted from a series of discoveries made by the natural sciences and all the related subjects on which the greatest intellects of our race have focused their attention in this marvelous period.

The laws, the physical phenomena, have always existed. In a real sense we have not invented these great developments. We have discovered them. They were always there. These great discoveries have other results. The wonders of transportation and of communication have expanded our interests to cover the whole world. What we do affects the whole world. What the whole world does affects us. This has great potentialities for good and for evil.

They have enormously multiplied material goods. The automobile, for example, as a useful device for the ordinary man, became possible as a result of a complex sum total of these discoveries derived from all the branches of science and engineering.

Again, we must see that this process may be used for good or evil, for the same complex web of discoveries and inventions makes either possible. It has made possible bigger and more destructive wars. Indeed, we have brought this development to the point where it threatens the destruction of our material civilization; and, being brought to that point, it threatens the same fate for intellectual and spiritual values as well.

It does this because we are leaving the moral problems unsolved. We are evading the question as to what we shall do with this great mass of discovery and invention. What they will do for us is of small importance as compared with the great question of what we will do with them. Let us narrow down our discussion to one of the problems that affect us as a nation.

We have had a year (1946) in which the nation has suffered from widespread and long-continued industrial strife. Industrial strife is not new. It has always broken out here and there in local disturbances for generations past. What is new is the greatly enlarged scale of its operations and effects. When great national unions come to a deadlock in their negotiations with great national industries, we have a condition which is no longer local. It affects us all. It works great harm to the people of the whole nation. Some of this harm is immediate and direct, while other results extend indirectly, but nonetheless seriously, over long periods of time and over great areas of the population. These great deadlocks between management and labor can no longer be directed solely against the parties to the dispute. They are directed against the well-being of the whole body of our citizens. Rebellion of the members, whose functions St. Paul so vividly described, hurts the whole body. The health of the members is only to be found in the health of the whole body.

One of the things St. Paul was writing about is the value and worth of every individual soul in the total mass of a great population like ours. The individual soul of the humblest citizen is the concern of the whole nation. The individual, likewise and in reverse, has a contribution which she or he can make to the well-being of the whole. This is Christian doctrine. It is not Nazi or Fascist doctrine, in which the interests of an imaginary body called the "state" is the ultimate object of human endeavor. Christian doctrine is that the State is charged with the welfare of the men, women, and children which compose it. The body's concern is with the health of its members; and the members, in turn, contribute to their own individual welfare and that of their fellows by doing their part to maintain the health of the body as a whole. How can we make this doctrine effective?

I venture to suggest that it will help us if we take a new view of our reasons for accepting Christian doctrine. We can accept it because it comes by revelation, but that may not be all there is in the matter that makes it demand our acceptance. Christian doctrine is not true solely because it has been revealed. It has been revealed because it is true.

We must be willing to see that throughout the history of mankind it has been found by those who observe life intently and clearly that, if men acted in certain ways, human relations were rich and satisfying. If they acted in other ways, man was set against man, the tremendous advantages of co-operation were lost, and valuable social institutions disintegrated.

The laws of the spiritual life which produced these results are universal laws applying to all mankind; and in studying them and discovering them, gleams of truth shone through the darkness in widely scattered corners of the earth and over millenniums of time.

This was a slow and painful process. What revelation has done is to present these laws simply and as a whole so that each civilization, each generation, and each person does not have to go himself through arduous trial and painful error to discover these things for himself. They have always been there, but by taking advantage of revelation, each person and the world can escape a mass of misery.

By thinking of these laws of life exclusively in terms of Christian revelation, we have done our society great harm. By considering them as laws of life existing eternally which revelation has made available to us, even as scientific discovery has made the ether waves available, we can perhaps make them more readily understood and more diligently followed. The damage that has been done is that, in considering them as the exclusive doctrine of a particular religion, we have eliminated them from the education of the young on the theory of the separation of the Church and the State. So long as they are considered to be the exclusive property of religious sects, rather than as being great universals whose rewards and penalties we can by no means escape, so long do we suffer the major part of our children to go out into life untaught and unprepared to face the most important facts of life.

The laws of Christian ethics are universally true. We must find means of reinstating their instruction into the training of the young. They must become the rules of loving for their elders. To bring this about is the great task of the Church, and this task must not be approached on the basis of sectarianism or from the standpoint of revelation alone. It must be approached as a task of instruction and practice in the fundamental laws of life.

St. Augustine's great pronouncement holds true: "Thou has made us for thyself and our lives are restless 'till they rest in thee." This truth comes to us with far more serious implications than in St. Augustine's simpler world. We live in a world far more dangerous, far more filled with possible material blessings, than his generation could possibly conceive. Let us begin now to teach and to live.

Tackling Negro-white Relationships

Lester B. Granger

THE PROBLEM of Negro-white relationships in this country is so vast and so complex that it is hopeless, in a brief discussion, to do more than cover one small phase of it. I prefer to discuss some of the emotional and economic factors that have operated historically to bring us to our present sad state, and to point out some practical steps that can be taken by interested groups today to ameliorate the worst aspects of the situation.

Racial relationships throughout the country are generally characterized by two opposing attitudes: a drive of Negroes for social and economic advancement, and a fear on the part of whites lest their prestige and security be involved in an upset of the status quo. The attitude of Negroes is a reflection of the new national alertness regarding the meaning and objectives of world democracy. Inspired by discussion of the Four Freedoms, Negroes have become acutely aware of their own exclusion from the provisions of these freedoms, and they want their citizenship place in American life redefined and lifted. Whites, on the other hand, are still narrowly provincial regarding their racial prejudices. They fail to see that the status of Negroes in this country is to many foreign peoples an indictment of our democratic professions toward the rest of the world. Neither have they been willing to accept the findings of science regarding racial differences and likenesses.

In other and even deeper ways, Negro-white relationships have poisoned our social standards and political life. The southern poll tax is the result of the South's determination to keep the vote away from the Negro citizen. And the poll tax has produced the reactionary, irresponsible, and ignorant Congressional bloc that has been our biggest barrier in the way of an efficient war program, just as it has blocked a hundred social reforms on which the majority of American citizens have been agreed. Racial prejudice and discrimination have wrecked the educational systems of a dozen southern states, and the whole nation pays the price in the inordinate amount of illiteracy, degeneracy, and crime which those states provide for us.

In cities like New York, a comparatively liberal community, we have had a chance to escape from the most serious of these errors. It is tragic that northern leadership has generally failed to take advantage of that chance. The growth of Harlem, the world's largest urban concentration of Negroes, is an example. A city of seven and one-half million persons has allowed itself to become frightened over an increasing Negro population which at the present time, amounts to less than half a million, five per cent of the total population. Negroes are neither the first nor the largest migrant group to "invade" the city. But they are the only group which today faces the

same problems, restrictions, and refusals of opportunities that met them upon their earliest arrival.
The usual "melting pot" process of acceptance, as-
similation, and integration has failed with respect
to the Negro, because more important to white
New York than the Negroes' cultural differences
and educational and economic lacks is their color
difference, and that difference is a permanent factor.
So, instead of landing at Ellis Island, settling in the
Lower East Side or Little Italy, and moving out in
the second generation to merge with the rest of the
population, Negroes have landed in Harlem to find
themselves and their children and their children's
children locked up for good in a black ghetto.

Just as residential segregation has limited living
opportunities and cheapened social values, so has
occupational discrimination lowered economic standards. Poor people who live in a poor neighborhood
and are kept poor are deprived of ambition outlets
and are cut off from normal cultural contact with the
rest of the city, and the inevitable result is a development of the slum psychology which is a new charac-
teristic of the Negro community. Nor is discrimination limited to housing and employment. Health
facilities and medical care are frequently denied to
the very group most in need of them. Recreational
services and guidance for youth are conspicuous by
their absence. Disorganization of family life follows
poverty, congestion, and unsavory neighborhood
influences. A persecution complex is encouraged
among the masses, and clever, unscrupulous leadership is always at hand to stimulate and take advantage of this spirit.

What has been said can describe Harlem in New York, or any of the large Negro neighborhoods in other metropolitan areas, or any of numerous "Harlems" throughout the country. Community leadership has an opportunity now to take stock of past failings and to chart a course of action for the future. Shall we be guided by the unscientific and socially disastrous fetishes and taboos that have been adopted by a former slave culture and have brought our Southern states to their present tragic pass? Or shall we be guided by the findings of science and the dictates of social ethics to avoid errors of the past and present? The decisions that we make today will decide which course we follow.

There is need today for a new interracial movement that is not dominated by whites acting in their own selfish interest, nor by Negroes too deeply preoccupied with their own troubles, but rather by white and Negro Americans who want first of all to build a real Christian democracy. Such a democracy will necessarily protect the interests of Negroes, because such protection is implicit in the true democratic concept. But such a democracy must start from the base of the general welfare. Negroes must be well-housed, because good housing for all is a requirement of civilized living. Job opportunities must be open on the basis of ability rather than race, because discrimination against one group automatically imperils the security of all. When we can get enough leaders of both races thinking along these lines, we shall have the basis for real co-operation between the races, which has no condescension or selfishness to mar its usefulness.

From this base we can launch our attack on housing, developing plans to rehabilitate obsolescent homes in which Negroes now live, find new land on which to develop new construction, make it possible for home buyers to purchase outside of the traditional Negro neighborhood. We can dare to offend superstitions and conventions of majority opinion, for we refuse to bow to any opinion which is so plainly set against the real public interest.

We are also able to look sanely and act courageously on the question of hospitalization and clinical service for Negroes, professional training and experience for nurses and physicians of their race. We refuse to go into hysterics over crime and disease rates among Negroes, recognizing that these are inevitable fruits of the social conditions we have nurtured in their neighborhoods. We let publication of shocking social statistics spur us to greater, not less, activity in behalf of a square deal for the Negro community.

These are some of the subjects that always come up for discussion of the "race problem." If Christian laymen cannot be depended upon for support of interracial co-operation and advancement of the Negro's status, then there is slight hope that the rest of America can be converted to the cause of building a real, living democracy. I hope that groups will take the problem home with them, bring it out for study of other groups to which they belong, and never rest until the Christian conscience shall so affect the organized Church that orthodox denominationalism may become an asset, rather than a hindrance, to this aspect of social progress.

Wider Horizons Are Yours

EDMUND D. AYRES

HOW WE ALL FRET AT TIMES at the tedium, drudgery, and monotony of daily living! There are periods when it seems that we cannot go on. Still, though we often complain, we rarely make any real attempt to escape from the deadening influences, to mind and spirit, of day after day of routine living. This, no doubt, is because we feel that this adventureless, humdrum existence is inevitable—the price we must pay for a "safe and sane" way of life. Actually, it is as if we had raised around us a wall, like a circle of string surrounding an anthill; and, antlike, we remain circumscribed by this self-limiting barrier. When we note this situation as it affects another, we readily agree that he has erred by trying to be sufficient unto himself; but, in our own case, we take refuge in the belief that we are helpless victims of circumstance!

There is, for most of us, only one escape from this vicious circle. We must recognize for ourselves, as for others, that no one of us was put here to live by himself; that no one stands still; and that, if we do not enlarge our sphere with new and fruitful human contacts, we shall find ourselves in a contracting circle; in short, that many of the inadequacies and dissatisfactions of daily living come from shutting the door of our mind and spirit on others.

This, of course, is not to suggest that thoughtless and indiscriminate contacts constitute the remedy for an "ingrowing personality," though we can say what wealth of experience and of stimulus may not reside, untapped, beneath the exterior of some casual acquaintance. The thought rather is that we should search out and be on the alert to recognize and respond to others who, like ourselves, are seeking to escape from stereotyped living. What keeps us from the adventure of making such new contacts? Inertia. The doubt that we shall find what we seek. The fear that the interests aroused by such contacts will absorb too much of our time and energy. The sad fact is that, instead of facing frankly these doubts and fears, and realizing what men of straw they often are, we let them shut the door on our "glimpse of the blue," and the succession of leaden skies continues.

There is no remedy for inertia better than an adoption of the adage, "Action will resolve the doubt which theory cannot solve." From the standpoint of sheer probability, we are at least as likely to discover kindred spirits as to be disappointed in our quest. The fear of expending too much time and energy fails to take into account the unused powers of personality, and the fact that sympathy expands as it is called upon. Beyond that is the expanding spirit of a group in search of wider horizons—a spirit that calls forth in each of its members a new dynamic viewpoint.

The group! History teems with examples of the solid achievements of small groups of men and women animated by like constructive purposes. Such a group it was that gave the Grecian Age of Pericles its imperishable fame. Such another group later calls the story of the gospel into alien lands, and helped give Christianity an impetus that has not spent its initial force in nearly twenty centuries!

Only the man who has associated himself with such a group can realize how rich an experience it is to work within the warmth of a circle, particularly one devoted to improving one's own response to human contacts. This warmth is not merely that which issues from a sharing of outlooks and problems. It comes from the group spirit itself. This spirit seems to arise spontaneously, to be generated in each group member, and, in turn, to broaden and deepen the viewpoint of each.

If the group is a congenial one, its interest in human relations almost can be taken for granted. Rarely, however, does such interest seek an intimate personal level. Rather, it concerns itself with a discussion of principles and examples, out of which more or less prosaic discussion emerges a sense of teamwork. This teamwork may seem merely to be the unexpressed meeting of minds. But, whatever the cause, the effect is to give each member the feeling that everyone is seeking to raise the level of his own actions. And this confidence in the motives of the other fellow makes the circle seem like some staunch and helpful disembodied spirit, which furnishes silent approval to all worthy successes in human contacts and softens the disappointing edge of failures. (Failures, of course, are often truer teachers than successes.) Personal reactions from this "trying" flow back to circle members, who find in them absorbing "case" material. Whether the circle

adopts group projects or the individual member
initiates his own, the feeling of group identification
with success or failure grows. As a result, a glow
from the sharing, in sympathy, of one's own efforts
permeates the circle.

Happiness in human relations is bound up, to a
considerable degree, with the adequate handling of
the multitude of human incidents that form the net-
work of our daily lives in office, shop, and home. To
attain this adequacy, the group is a major help in the
way it builds into one's mind a store of principles,
along with their effective application in a number
of varying incidents. When a member of the circle
is confronted with an unexpected human problem,
there comes to mind, out of this store, a solution
that, in discussion, worked well under somewhat
similar circumstances. Thus, a sudden situation can
be handled with a reasonable degree of confidence;
and, more and more, the automatic response to a
situation can be relied upon as springing from a
richer and richer background of correct principles
and positive attitudes. Certainly, a more valuable
benefit than this conditioning of the individual by
the group could scarcely be obtained at any price or
in any other way.

The trend of such a circle to raise the standard of
mental living of its members comes about in a very
natural, though unexpected, way. Group discussions
grapple sooner or later with human problems that
cannot be separated from such factors as individual
faith in God and the practice of Christianity, making
it both necessary and desirable to take such factors
into account in any solutions. Divorced from all

"isms," the place and importance of these spiritual approaches become clearer to most of us than they ever have been before, as essential "vitamins" of daily living. Soon, the need for greater firsthand knowledge and inspiration makes itself felt. Without further encouragement, each member of the circle finds himself almost automatically taking steps to supply this need by reading novels with inspirational subjects or characters, more Bible study, more frequent attendance at church, some daily devotional program, or some other personally satisfying method. This trend, occurring in a group whose leaders have decided against discussion of religion in any form, is of "eye-opening" interest.

Once this natural development occurs, individual and group projects begin to border on experiments in Christian living, and the richness and satisfaction of individual and group experience become greatly enhanced. The spontaneity and power of this urge in a group marked by heterogeneity in religious background confirms the belief that the circle is both a basic and a natural way to interest the ordinary man or woman in getting "in tune with the Infinite." It also suggests that greater courage and strength for the practice of Christian principles in everyday life can be freely drawn from the human and spiritual resources of laymen groups. Life takes on a new significance that is priceless to the individual and the potentialities for good possessed by such groups suggest the way to a better America.

II

The Layman in His Personal Life

A Satisfied Customer

JOHN P. HOLMES

WE WILL ALL AGREE that something is wrong with our modern world. The chief problems we face are not the problems of making peace, great as these are. This is because the war was only a symptom of the sickness of our civilization. We need to devote ourselves to the task of spiritual reconstruction and put thought into elaboration of an adequate faith rather than into a new machine. We need so to combine scientific and technical skill with moral and spiritual discipline that the products of human genius shall be used for the good of the human race rather than its destruction. The answer seems to me to be a reaffirmation of the Christian faith. This faith can best be nourished by the organized Church and a fellowship of active laymen.

I am a salesman by trade. I am trying to practice Christianity and, in the language of my trade, I am a "satisfied customer." While I was reared in a Christian home and environment, I, for some reason, never consciously tried to practice Christianity in my everyday life until the last few years. I do not feel that I have gotten very far but I have received a dividend of satisfaction from walking in the right direction. Christianity is a practical way of life and I have found that it works. We need not comply with

a time schedule in order to practice Christianity.
The time is now and the place is just where we are.
God has been seeking us from the beginning. Our
responsibility, then, is one of responding. I like to
think that God is always ready to meet anyone half-
way. But learning to respond to God is, in itself,
not as easy an experience as I once thought. Most
men like myself have used God and religion in emer-
gencies only. The result has been that most of the
time we have run our lives without the benefit of
his help or approval.

When a man has spent a large part of his adult life
without a conscious effort to know God's will, he will
find it a hard task to change. But it can be done. If
we would but set aside, say, one-half hour each day,
and spend this time in meditation and prayer, I am
sure that God would gradually reveal himself and
his plans to us and our lives would then have new
meaning and a new sense of direction. This material
universe of ours is controlled by the moral and
spiritual laws of God, and it is necessary that we spend
time in getting to know something of the nature of
God and our relationship to him.

One of our greatest sources of information con-
cerning the nature and will of God is found in the
revelation of God through the life and teaching of
Jesus. Each time I reread and study the New Testament, I find new revelations. If we are willing to
dedicate our lives and surrender self, we will find
new strength and companionship in the Risen and
Living Christ.

Let me speak briefly of my experience with the
practice of Christianity in business, family, and

church relations. In so far as my business activities are concerned, I can find no conflict between business and Christianity. A really successful business, whether we realize it or not, must be built on Christian principles. I think that Christ is the greatest economist that ever lived, and unless the business of the future is based on Christ's teachings, then it is destined to fail. Christ promised freedom and maximum profits in both spiritual and material riches to all who would follow his economic teaching. What other economist ever promised as much? It is the disregard of the principle of the Golden Rule through greed and the lust of conquest, by a few small minorities, that has brought about the present conflict and misunderstandings between capital and labor. The problem of human relations brought about by mass production will become even more acute in the postwar world unless a better system of economy is worked out, based on the laws of human conduct set down in Christ's teachings.

Many of the new scientific developments and products of modern business will actually become a curse instead of a blessing, unless given the proper spiritual and moral direction.

Certainly I think we will all agree that our family relations or a happy home are of the utmost importance. If we have been blessed with children, it is of even greater importance. Now one simply cannot hope to have a truly happy home based on anything else than the practice of Christian principles as set forth in the Golden Rule. I do not think one can set down hard and fast rules, as conditions in every family are different, but I do think it very important that some kind of family worship be held, particularly when there are children. Young lives are formed, not chiefly by the intellectual beliefs of their parents, of which they may be wholly ignorant, but far more by family practices, such as attendance at church, family worship, etc., which become habitual and are eventually unconscious influences of incalculable importance. We have found it very helpful in our family to have a short service at breakfast each morning. There are a number of books available which will be helpful in conducting a short service, such as *Two Minutes with God,* by Hoh and Hoh. Such a service in the morning sets the theme for the day and is helpful in creating the proper atmosphere. There are many other things which might be done, for example, a short family-worship service Sunday evening, reading of Bible stories to the children, etc. I can certainly say from experience that since my wife and I have tried to build our home in the proper relationship to God, that it has been a much happier place in which to live.

We hear much about juvenile delinquency; we can at least meet the challenge for action by starting in our own homes. We spend a great deal of time and money teaching our children all about our modern world, but we make almost no effort to give them a living knowledge of the spiritual sources of our civilization. Is it no wonder that our children have no desire to go to Sunday School and that discipline is a problem? We as parents are not showing our children, by example and deed in our everyday lives, the importance of Christianity and the spiritual values of life. This is something we as laymen can and must do if we are to have a better world in which to live.

With reference to my relations to the Church, I would like to say that I owe a debt of gratitude to the Church and the clergy that I can never repay. I do feel, however, that the Church is not demanding enough of its laymen. If the world is to be changed, then I feel that the ministers should solicit the help of its laymen, and the laymen should do everything in their power to strengthen the Church. The Church should better organize its laymen into groups according to their needs and give them the training and spiritual preparation necessary for them to become active in carrying on the work of the Church. This can best be done under the leadership of the minister and it is a challenge to the clergy to solicit the help of the laymen in deepening the spiritual lives of its members and making the Church become a more active and dynamic force for good in the community. The Church of Christ will never die but it will move faster in attaining its goal if it would rally its laymen into more active service.

Beginning Religion

BY A YOUNG BUSINESS EXECUTIVE

"ARE YOU ONE OF THESE DO-GOODERS who believes in God?" The question came abruptly in the course of a conversation with a professional woman with whom I was working as a volunteer aid in a social service project. On another occasion a business associate to whom I spoke of a recent religious conference responded half jokingly, "Don't tell me you've gone religious!" The shortest and most accurate answer in each case could easily have been a very modest, "Yes." However, the questions demanded a "yes, because" answer, and both times I was practically tongue-tied on account of what seemed to be the appalling difficulty of making my position intelligible in the face of such skepticism.

The fault was largely in me. I believe that each of these persons could have been led to understand my attitude and to accept it as at least on the safe side of lunacy if I had been at all prepared to explain myself. Their secularism is my own tradition, and I still know and, most of the time, use their language. Certainly I should be able to explain to them the changes that are occurring in my thinking and, very gradually, in my way of living. Because I owe a decent answer to such questions, I have tried to frame it in this statement. It is necessarily a personal narrative.

Like everyone else, I have been looking consciously or otherwise for happiness. I started out in adolescence subscribing fully to the current doctrine that happiness was to be found through a well-balanced development in work, play, aesthetic interests, and human relationships. Each promised a reward. Work offered an adequate income, satisfaction of accomplishment, and sometimes prestige. Play meant fun and gaiety. Among the arts, music gave me special pleasure in appreciation and, to a modest degree, in performance as well. In people one found emotional response, and I hoped for spiritual completion eventually in marriage. Religion, as a personal function, was outside my scheme of things. It might have its psychological uses for those who failed in life, but I saw no need for it. I believed in personal adequacy as a practical goal. Barring a stupid accident, I saw no reason why I should ever fail in anything important to me. Moreover, I strongly suspected that the strength and comfort which people gained from religion was largely the result of auto-suggestion.

At no time was this philosophy ever completely successful, and as I advanced into adulthood it became less and less satisfactory. The years brought increasing ambition and consequent strain, together with a recognition that choices of attitudes and action were becoming irrevocable. Yet I seemed to be less and less happy. There were experiences of failure. They were never catastrophic; indeed the failure usually consisted only in lesser success than I had aimed at. Nevertheless, my optimism was shaken. Further, I also discovered that the satisfaction of

realized successes seldom came up to my expecta-
tions. My utmost in effort and discipline was re-
warded by only a fleeting thrill of achievement which
soon turned to boredom. Thus it developed that an
earlier assurance of happiness gradually gave ground
to a dismal alteration between the sting of failure
and the frustration of unsatisfying success.

Such an experience is, I suspect, a well-trodden
highway to the narrower path of religion. Fortunately my discomfort was sufficiently acute to impel
me to go on. In the transition I had some assistance
at first from two utilitarian precepts which were
not too offensive to my rationalism. One was that
success is measured not by one's endowment but by
his use of it. The other was that happiness is only
to be found through unselfish devotion and not by
direct conquest. I was obviously obliged to scale
down my ambition to my apparent abilities, and I
was willing to try to direct it to ends beyond my own
gratification. This latter adjustment was the more
difficult one. It at least made sense from the point
of view of social ethics, and, besides, the psychologists
had discovered that the self-seeking ego had in it
much that was cruel and destructive, even self-
destructive. However, disciplined altruism under-
taken for its own sake or as the lesser of evils holds
only the grim comfort of stoical achievement. I came
to realize that it could succeed psychologically only
if it were supported and motivated by a genuine, self-
effacing love. That quality seemd almost entirely
lacking in my make-up.

It was a painful predicament as I came to realize
it more and more fully. Egocentricity is undoubtedly

the most awful form of human isolation. Any real
experience of companionship, of human affinity, is
precluded. There is only the self amidst a world
inevitably hostile to its demands. Even if in despera-
tion one turns to God, there seems to be no response.
One can pray to God only if he loves God.

"God resisteth the proud, and giveth grace to the
humble." I had relied exclusively on self-centered,
secular thinking in adjusting to life. It had brought
me to an impasse, which fortunately I recognized
fully enough so that I was, in spite of myself, humbled. I was humbled to the extent that I was willing
to listen to the person who now and again spoke of
the joys of his faith. The faith seemed to me to be
based on assumptions which were unsupportable
logically, for my education and my inheritance of
so-called common sense indicated a world functioning mechanically according to impersonal laws which
left no room for divine intervention. However, it
became more and more apparent that an illogical
faith was much more satisfactory to live with and by
than a logical despair.

Finally, in a book by Gerald Heard, *The Third
Morality*, came the suggestion that the nature and
meaning of existence were inadequately, even falsely,
indicated by the superficial testimony of everyday
material perception and so-called common sense;
that in fact the whole mechanistic philosophy, though
it might flatter the reasoning ego with a specious ap-
pearance of completeness and mathematical certainty, was actually at variance with findings of bolder
(and also humbler) minds in the vanguard of scientific research. In short, I discovered that my ra-

tional difficulties, so-called, with a spiritual interpretation of life were themselves based on ignorance.
The Spirit, of course, is not a supernatural personality which can be propitiated and cajoled into
opportune deflection of natural laws on my behalf.
(It does, however, at least now and again, appear
lovingly in my personality and in other personalities.) It is the Source and Goal, the Source from
which I can receive assurance and strength, and the
Goal from which I can derive meaning and incentive.
It is the ultimate in Love, Power, Truth, Perfection
to which somehow, miraculously, I am given access.
It is the Reality beyond reality which is both immi-
nent and transcendent.

The implications of such a discovery are pro-
foundly significant. It means that the one important
satisfaction is to love, to serve, and finally to know
God. The world's end, business success, wealth, even
the good opinion of others, become largely irrelevant,
if not downright undesirable as distractions. Furthermore, to love God must mean to trust him; but
to trust God means to devalue one's own opinions
to the level of tentative speculations and to accept
drastic limitations on one's own personal responsibility. One cannot put his trust in God and regard
himself at the same time as the master of his own
destiny. Again, one cannot love God and hate his
creatures. Absolute charity and love toward all crea-
tion are necessarily implied in loving God.

The pattern is clear and consistent as I write. But
let me go out to resume for just a few hours the
everyday activities of work and pleasure, and then
return and check my performance against these speci-

fications. The results are appalling. I find that I have yielded again and again to the lure of personal ambition, to vanity, even in my good deeds. I have worried and fretted about my undertakings as though I really considered myself solely responsible. I have attempted to force my will on other people. I have felt and expressed resentment at the stupidity and faults of others. Forgetting God and indulging my self-love, I have given the lie almost wholly to what I say I believe. In fact, the strength of the belief itself has faded. God seems remote, and I am beset with doubts.

Obviously the new relief calls at the outset for a fundamental alteration of conduct, attitudes, and character. For me, and I suspect for most of us, it is a tremendously difficult undertaking. It can only be accomplished by deliberate and sustained training. Here, again, I have been greatly indebted to the books of Gerald Heard for advice and encouragement. Daily meditation is fundamental. At first it was a considerable effort. I chose the half hour between dressing and breakfast, and at the outset I could do little more than repeat some prayers with superficial interest and attention. Often there was no comfort at all. Now, after a year and a half, although the content of my meditations is still evolving, this daily experience has become increasingly significant and important to me.

Usually I prepare myself by reading briefly in any one of several source books. The first part of the meditation itself is a sort of orientation, perhaps taking the form of listing some of the attributes of the Spirit which I would worship, or of recounting to

myself my reasons for loving God. Often my efforts
at the outset seem a vain repetition of words, and
I know then that I must wait for God's help in
identifying and purging the attitude somewhere in
the back of my mind which is standing in my way.
Nowadays the helpful insight usually comes, after
a while, in the form of a confession which is followed by sorrow, repentance, and an earnest petition
for forgiveness. By this time I come naturally to a
kind of dedication. It takes the form of a chain
prayer, a series of thoughts and expressions which
I have acumulated over a rather long period of time.
It is all summed up in a slow and thoughtful repetition, phrase by phrase of the Lord's Prayer. Finally,
I sit with a feeling of being somehow close to God,
and I like at this time to think of God's love as it
might and as I hope it will be expressed in and for
different people whom I know.

During the day I attempt from time to time to
return to some of the thoughts of this early morning
period. It is difficult, and I am not very often successful. Nevertheless I can try at least to avoid
attitudes and acts which I identify as hostile to my
dedication of the morning. Reading, even in occasional snatches, can be an aid to one's training, and
fortunately the literature, both old and new, is
abundant and rich. Conversation and companionship with another person of similar aspirations are
a great satisfaction, and they can contribute power-
fully to the vividness and vitality of one's private devotion for days afterward. Writing in letters or in a
journal can be helpful in clarifying and sharpening
one's belief and dedication.

These I consider the special techniques of spiritual training. In my case they are carried on simultaneously with an active business and social life, and I feel that my progress in the future must be measured in large part by the extent to which I can integrate this life with the thoughts and aspirations of my private devotions. Thus far I have not discovered any necessary conflict between the two, although, as I have already indicated, I find that I continually create unnecessary conflicts by failing to carry over from the one frame of existence to the other. To be sure, the environment of the private profit system lends itself to wrong attitudes of selfish exploitation, but so does nearly every human situation. On the other hand, there is no reason beyond myself why I cannot function in society as it is now constituted and at the same time achieve at least a greatly improved quality of being. Anything beyond that, any state aproaching perfection in this world, is so far beyond my present capacity that I need not, now at least, worry about it.

Getting back to the questions which prompted this account, I arrive at these answers: "I have 'gone religious' because I believe that my personal fulfilment, my only real possibility of happiness, lies in increasing love and service and knowledge of God. I have made a start in this direction, a very small one, but I know there is hope in training, for God helps those who seek him. Best of all, perhaps, I have had a glimpse of the joys of the dedicated life."

How Men Respond to Religion

Weyman C. Huckabee

I HAVE FOUND that men are fundamentally different in their response to religion. The present program of the Church, which provides the same spiritual diet for all alike in the form of the Sunday morning service, may have to be altered if this difference in men is met.

There are at least two responses which men have to religion. The first of these is found in men who have unusual capacity for effective prayer and meditation. They are by nature sensitive to spiritual values. They possess a hunger for God which other men cannot fully understand, and for this reason they are often misunderstood and discredited. They have a migratory urge to respond to the pull of God, though it may be poorly, or in the beginning not at all, expressed. A businessman who is a "meditative" described his experience in this way: "When in the depth of secularism a few years ago, I found myself deeply moved one day while reading about the response of the saints to the call of God."

Things of the moment are likely to mean less to a person of this type. If he will let himself go he will find that he cares deeply because God, to some extent, is negated by his disbelief and the disbelief of others around him.

The "meditative," as he begins to develop, is able to carry a powerful spiritual charge, which is capable of creating good will among great numbers of men. Yet his very nature is such that he is the first to deny that he possesses any unusual ability.

Such men would be of great value to the Church and to society at large if only they could be sought out and encouraged to develop. Unfortunately they, like chronic alcoholics, find it difficult to get "identification" with anyone who isn't of their type, in this case a "meditative"; and "meditatives" are as scarce among ministers as they are among laymen.

The second general type is much easier to spot. He is a person of action. When first found he seems to have little capacity for a deeply spiritual life. He is driven by an urge, which the "meditative" finds difficult to understand, to put his convictions immediately into action. The "active" believes that he, with a little help from God, can create a decent society. The "meditative," on the other hand, feels that God will bring such a society into being with only a little help from men. Because of this difference of emphasis upon man's importance, the "meditative" and the "active" are inclined to get on each other's nerves and to discount the fine qualities of each.

What practical proposals can be made? We, regardless of our type, can look within ourselves and find what interest we have in God and his purpose for our lives and the lives of our fellow men.

This is exactly what has happened to a group of men whom I know. Something new and different is stirring in their lives. It is, I believe, the workings

of God—perhaps as yet only a vague understanding
of his purpose, but nevertheless it is real. The fact
that this new interest is not restricted to one area
or to men within or without the Church or to Protestants or Catholics leads me to feel that what they are
finding out about God, inadequate as it still may be,
is not due to any special or peculiar gift or situation
limited to them. If God can stir their lives to a new
sense of need of him and a new sense of obligation
to their fellow man, he can stir any man's life, for it
is what is common in all of us that responds to God.

For the man beginning the development of his
Christian life, the practice of "alternation" is essential. In the same manner he would begin any new
habit, he should at regular intervals turn his thoughts
in God's direction, and then in the direction of the
needs of his fellow men. This is a matter, I believe,
in which there is no choice if right action is to be
followed. He must learn to receive from God, then
learn immediately how to give what he receives to
his fellow men.

After this practice is started, instructions for further development will vary, depending upon whether
one is inclined to be a "meditative" or an "active."
The "meditative" will require fellowship in prayer,
particularly silent prayer. As a beginner he should
be encouraged to study devotional books.

He will need instructions in what to do when "the
dark night of the soul" comes. He will need help
when he begins, in a serious way, to practice intercessory prayer. The time may come when his prayers
become the end rather than the means of achieving

a full Christian life. He must be shown the dangers of "spiritual pride."

The "active" must come face to face with the fact that deeds that are separated from contact with God are of little value, as compared with services rendered to others as a result of devotion to God and his purpose. His restless soul must take on the discipline of periods of devotion to God at regular intervals. He must come to know how many hours he can be active as a Christian in secular affairs before he must renew his mind in God's presence. He of all men must watch pride. It is not easy for an "active" to be humble, he has so many natural abilities. He must learn that the real source of power for his activities is found only by those who are trained in the life of the spirit. He will profit by the study of such books as: *The Sayings of Jesus* and *The Return to Religion,* by H. C. Link, *In Search of Maturity,* by Fritz Kunkel, *A Testament of Devotion,* by T. R. Kelly, *Prayer and Worship,* by D. V. Steere, *Abundant Living,* by Stanley Jones, and *In Quest of a Kingdom,* by Leslie D. Weatherhead.

One temptation of the "meditative" will be to pray with little or no thought given to the necessity of his working in the groups in society which have a claim on his time and interest. While the "active" will find that his temptation is to rush in unassisted by God to cure any ill, actually the "meditative," as he develops, will need to be warned against overdoing the cultivation of the inner life, if at the same time he is failing to discover practical ways of expressing his concern for his fellow men. "For he that loveth not his brother whom he hath seen, how can he love God whom he hath not seen?" Yet the "active" will need to control his tendency to "take over" the situation before he has met the conditions which are demanded before God can qualify him.

It is not simple to receive gifts from God. There are conditions which God and our souls demand which we can learn only by trial and error and by discipline. Yet, I know that it is down that road many more of us must travel. Most of us have never disciplined ourselves to pray. Our chief concern has not been to know and do God's will at any cost in small or large decisions. The selfishness, pride, and ambition which are in us have been the filters through which most of our "messages" from God have come. To rid ourselves of these hindrances seems at times next to impossible.

One practice we should learn is what Gerald Heard calls the prayer of "simple attention." How easy it is to pray with words. We can be proud in audible prayer but how humble one must be who waits in silence before God, feeling a deep need but denying himself the right to ask for help. But it is difficult to concentrate on being in God's presence. One or two minutes at a time is about all a beginner can achieve before his mind darts off to chase an idea that has crashed through. This again is where discipline comes in.

Giving to my fellow man is equally difficult. To do it without desire for credit, the only gift I can imagine God accepting, is very difficult. How wonderful it would be if one could be an anonymous Christian. But the ego won't let us. All we can do is to try, in spite of the fact that our failures will likely outnumber our successes. But we may be sure that it is the struggle along this road which gives meaning to life.

Men can be taught, in a fashion, how to pray. With less difficulty they can be taught to act, to agitate for social reform, do good works, and serve others. With even greater ease they can be taught to contribute money to a worthy cause. But none of these is adequate. A still more difficult thing is required, that is, to practice prayer—prayer that is an earnest effort by men to come into God's presence and to obey him; then immediately give expression, in the common everyday experiences, to that which is created when man meets God.

The most essential thing then, and the most difficult thing we Christians are called upon to do, is to build a bridge for two-way passage between our prayers and our daily activities. The man who begins to pray and is not more considerate of his family, friends, and business associates, more aware of discriminations and injustices and of his personal obligation to work for a Christian society, needs further assistance in developing his prayer life. It is not, therefore, really a matter of praying more and doing less or doing more and praying less. It is a matter of prayed action, or action that is first prayed.

A thoughtful person is startled by the fact that a few men who begin to cultivate a life of action centered in God are effective altogether out of proportion to their numbers. Three or four such men, I believe, will gradually change a dry, ineffective church or community into a dynamic one. They will do the same with any group, whether it be religious, social, political, or business. I firmly believe that this kind of living offers the only solution to problems that grow out of bad human relations, and it isn't easy to name a problem the root of which isn't found in some man or group of men.

In conclusion, I venture to give two examples. One of these is a young executive who has achieved success in business. Three years ago he was an average, indifferent layman as far as church affiliation or interest in religion in any form was concerned. He says now he does not know what started his thinking along a different line. He would be the first to deny that very much progress has been made thus far but I know the road down which he is traveling. He is definitely a "meditative." His daily companions are books such as *The Imitation of Christ* and those by Evelyn Underhill, Gerald Heard, and Douglas Steere. He seeks continuous contact with God, though admitting repeated failures. As this growth from within has developed he has become identified with the Church, becoming a trustee and an elder. He and his wife have been meeting regularly, for two years, with a few others who are interested in the development of their spiritual lives. He is only a beginner, but his decision to experiment with the religious life has made him of much more value these last few months to his business, his community, his church, and his home.

The other example is also a young executive about the same age and equally successful. He is definitely an "active." His conviction is that a man has no right to pray until he has first exhausted his natural abilities to solve the problems at hand. The life of the so-called "meditative" seems to him to be a mistake. It is his belief that when such practices are emphasized men are stymied by the receiving end of religion, and problems which demand immediate solutions are neglected. Prayer to him is very important, but one earns by his work the right to pray. All one needs to do is to admit he is unable to do a certain job without God's help, then he has only to ask. This man has worked continuously the past two years to apply Christianity in his everyday affairs and has been a source of inspiration to hundreds of others.

These men are developing according to their natural response to religion. They are starting where they are, with what they have, and as they grow they will come to have an increased respect for each other. They will come to see that they are two sides of the same shield.

Micah and Jesus have given us the steps which are to be taken if religion is to be made the source of power for our daily lives. Micah says: "He hath showed, thee, O man, what is good; and what doth the Lord require of thee, but to do justly, and to love mercy, and to walk humbly with thy God."

Jesus says: "The first of all commandments is, Hear, O Israel; The Lord our God is one Lord; and thou shalt love the Lord thy God with all thy heart, and with all thy soul, and with all thy mind, and with all thy strength; this is the first commandment. And the second is like unto it, namely this, Thou shalt love thy neighbor as thyself. There is none other commandment greater than these."

A Miracle across the Kitchen Table

BY ONE OF THE FOUNDERS OF ALCOHOLICS ANONYMOUS

SOMEONE HAS SAID, I think with a great deal of
power, "God grant me the serenity to accept
the things I cannot change, courage to change the
things I can, and wisdom to know the difference."
But an alcoholic is a man in whom neither courage,
serenity, nor wisdom is present.

My own experience came to me in this way. I had
run out the string to such a point that a doctor told
my wife eight years ago last summer that I could not
live, or if I did, not with my sanity. For two or
three years prior to that sad summer day when she
was told this, I had tried desperately to stop drinking. Before it really got me I had had some will
power, which I now look back on as obstinacy. A
good physician said I had an allergy of the body—
an obsession that would insure my keeping on drinking. He recommended to my wife that I be shut up,
as that was the only way I could live. I was powerless to go on; although I had not been told in so
many words, I knew that it had to come to that.

No words can tell of the loneliness and despair I
found in that bitter morass of self-pity. Quicksand
stretched around me in all directions. I had met my
match. I had been overwhelmed. Alcohol was my
master.

Near the end of that bleak November, I sat drinking in my kitchen. With a certain satisfaction I reflected there was enough gin concealed about the house to carry me through that night and the next day. My wife was at work. I wondered whether I dared hide a full bottle of gin near the head of our bed. I would need it before daylight.

My musing was interrupted by the telephone. The cheery voice of an old school friend asked if he might come over. He was sober. It was years since I could remember his coming to New York in that condition. I was amazed.

The door opened and he stood there, fresh-skinned and glowing. There was something about his eyes. He was inexplicably different. What had happened?

I pushed a drink across the table. He refused it. Disappointed but curious, I wondered what had got into the fellow. He wasn't himself.

"Come, what's all this about?" I queried.

He looked straight at me. Simply, but smilingly, he said, "I've got religion."

I was aghast. So that was it—last summer an alcoholic crackpot; now, I suspected, a little cracked about religion. He had that starry-eyed look. Yes, the old boy was on fire all right. But bless his heart, let him rant! Besides, my gin would last longer than his preaching.

But he did no ranting. In a matter-of-fact way he told how two men had appeared in court, persuading the judge to suspend his commitment. They had told of a simple religious idea and a practical program of action. That was two months ago and the result was self-evident. It worked!

He had come to pass his experience along to me —if I cared to have it. I was shocked, but interested. Certainly I was interested. I had to be, for I was hopeless.

I had always believed in a power greater than myself. I had often pondered these things. I was not an atheist. Few people really are, for that means blind faith in the strange proposition that this universe originated in a cipher and aimlessly rushes nowhere. My intellectual heroes, the chemists, the astronomers, even the evolutionists, suggested vast laws and forces at work. Despite contrary indication, I had little doubt that a mighty purpose and rhythm underlay all. How could there be so much of precise and immutable law, and no intelligence? I simply had to believe in a Spirit of the Universe, who knew neither time nor limitation. But that was as far as I had gone.

With ministers, and the world's religions, I parted right there. When they talked of a God, personal to me, who was love, superhuman strength, and direction, I became irritated, and my mind snapped shut against such a theory.

To Christ I conceded the certainty of a great man, not too closely followed by those who claimed him. His moral teaching—most excellent. For myself, I had adopted those parts which seemed convenient and not too difficult; the rest I disregarded.

But my friend sat before me, and he made the point-blank declaration that God had done for him what he could not do for himself. His human will had failed. Doctors had pronounced him incurable. Society was about to lock him up. Like myself, he had admitted complete defeat. Then he had, in effect, been raised from the dead, suddenly taken from the scrap heap to a level of life better than the best he had ever known!

Had this power originated in him? Obviously it had not. There had been no more power in him than there was in me at that minute; and this was none at all.

That floored me. It began to look as though religious people were right after all. Here was something at work in a human heart which had done the impossible. My ideas about miracles were drastically revised right then. Never mind the musty past; here sat a miracle directly across the kitchen table. He shouted great tidings.

My friend suggested what then seemed a novel idea. He said: "Why don't you choose your own conception of God?"

That statement hit me hard. It melted the icy intellectual mountain in whose shadow I had lived and shivered many years. I stood in the sunlight at last.

It was only a matter of being willing to believe in a power greater than myself. Nothing more was required of me to make my beginning. I saw that growth could start from that point. Upon a foundation of complete willingness I might build what I saw in my friend. Would I have it? Of course I would!

Thus was I convinced that God is concerned with us humans when we want him enough. At long last I saw, I felt, I believed. Scales of pride and prejudice fell from my eyes. A new world came into view.

At the hospital I was separated from alcohol for

the last time. Treatment seemed wise, for I showed signs of delirium tremens.

There I humbly offered myself to God, as I then understood him, to do with me as he would. I placed myself unreservedly under his care and direction. I admitted for the first time that of myself I was nothing, that without him I was lost. I ruthlessly faced my sins and became willing to have my new-found Friend take them away, root and branch. I have not had a drink since.

My schoolmate visited me, and I fully acquainted him with my problems and deficiencies. We made a list of people I had hurt or toward whom I felt resentment. I expressed my entire willingness to approach these individuals, admitting my wrong. Never was I to be critical of them. I was to right all such matters to the utmost of my ability.

I was to test my thinking by the new God consciousness within. Common sense would thus become uncommon sense. I was to sit quietly when in doubt, asking only for direction and strength to meet my problems as he would have me. Never was I to pray for myself, except as my requests bore on my usefulness to others. Then only might I expect to receive. But that would be in great measure.

My friend promised when these things were done I would enter upon a new relationship with my Creator; that I would have the elements of a way of living which answered all my problems. Belief in the power of God, plus enough willingness, honesty, and humility to establish and maintain the new order of things, were the essential requirements.

Simple, but not easy; a price had to be paid. It

meant destruction of self-centeredness. I must turn in all things to the Father of Lights who presides over us all.

There were revolutionary and drastic proposals, but the moment I fully accepted them, the effect was electric. There was a sense of victory, followed by such a peace and serenity as I had never known. There was utter confidence. I felt lifted up, as though the great clean wind of a mountaintop blew through and through. God comes to most men gradually, but his impact on me was sudden and profound.

For a moment I was alarmed and called my friend, the doctor, to ask if I were still sane. He listened in wonder as I talked.

Finally he shook his head saying, "Something has happened to you I don't understand. But you had better hang on to it. Anything is better than the way you were."

After my release my wife and I abandoned ourselves with enthusiasm to the idea of helping other alcoholics to a solution of their problems. It was fortunate, for my old business associates remained skeptical for a year and a half, during which time I found little work. I was not too well at the time, and was plagued by waves of self-pity and resentment. This sometimes nearly drove me back to drink. I soon found that when all other measures failed, work with another alcoholic would save the day. Many times I have gone to my old hospital in despair. On talking to a man there, I would be amazingly lifted up and set on my feet. It is a design for living that works in rough going.

We commenced to make many fast friends, and a fellowship has grown up among us in Alcoholics Anonymous of which it is a wonderful thing to feel a part. The joy of living we really have, even under pressure and difficulty! I have seen hundreds of families set their feet in the path that really goes somewhere; have seen the most impossible domestic situations righted, feuds and bitterness of all sorts wiped out. I have seen men come out of asylums and resume a vital place in the lives of their families and communities. Business- and professional men have regained their standing. There is scarcely any form of trouble and misery which has not been overcome among us.

The members of Alcoholics Anonymous have tried to look scientifically at the factors in their cure. When science tries to transform the human person what does it say: personality change absolutely necessary; analysis of personality and catharsis; realistic facing of the problem plus disciplined attack upon them; maladjusted personality violates hard instinct.

We have also tried to analyze the approach of religion. Religion says: a spiritual awakening is necessary, a change of heart; suggests being honest with myself, frank discussions, an examination of the causes; program of adjustment, unselfish service, love; fault is in self-centeredness—remember each is a part of the brotherhood of man.

Both science and religion insist that the person desiring the transformation must find a new compelling influence.

Alcoholics Anonymous has combined religion and science and has added: a common state of being which gives identification, and a consuming new interest in helping one another. To science it adds the necessity of belief in God and the practice of prayer. To religion, which says have faith in God, it adds the daily necessity of helping another alcoholic.

A prayer often used by Alcoholics Anonymous is the prayer of St. Francis:

> O Lord, our Christ, may we have thy mind and thy spirit; make us instruments of thy peace; where there is hatred, let us sow love; where there is injury, pardon; where there is discord, union; where there is doubt, faith; where there is despair, hope; where there is darkness, light; and where there is sadness, joy. O divine Master, grant that we may not so much seek to be consoled as to console; to be understood, as to understand; to be loved, as to love; for it is in giving that we receive; it is in pardoning that we are pardoned; and it is in dying that we are born to eternal life. *Amen.*

A Businessman's Search for God

A. Ludlow Kramer

MY LIFE, as seen from the outside, was conventional and uninteresting. I was energetic, ambitious, proud, self-seeking, conceited, and self-willed. These qualities take us sometimes a long way in our life in the world, and I secured every worldly thing I had ever wanted. I became a businessman, and retired at the age of thirty-eight to devote the balance of my life to travel, sports, and study. I was pretty well satisfied with myself.

I was not, however, really happy, certainly not continuously so. I had occasional moments of great happiness, but they were fleeting and entirely dependent on others. As the years rolled on, I became less happy. I hardly knew why. I always seemed to be wanting something, and often did not know just what it was.

I turned to philosophy and read about everything one could obtain on this subject. The last writers seemed to agree with Plato, so it seemed to me that we had been having debates for two thousand years and were back where we started.

Then I studied psychology and found it a fascinating hobby. I cannot claim to have loved people at this time, but I was tremendously interested in them, and many life histories were laid bare to me. I helped to solve many problems, although I realize now that I took the responsibility of decisions I should not have taken. I finally got to a point where I was doing original research, and discovered the cause of paralysis resulting from "shock" or "shell shock." I think that this discovery contains valuable lessons. It shows the desirability of our being honest with ourselves. Indeed, it shows that tragedy may result if we are not.

If a man is afraid and acknowledges the fear to himself, he may have a conflict between his ideals and his instinct for self-preservation, which may be decided either way; but he will not suffer from shock. On the other hand, if he does not acknowledge this fear, but represses it, he is apt to be a victim of shock. Unacknowledged emotions of any kind tend to multiply and may cause havoc to our nervous systems.

I came to realize that if I was to be a practical psychologist I must explore for myself instead of spending my time in a "highchair" trying to interpret the experiences of others. Eventually, I learned that God gives us the humility and courage to do this if we call upon him to do so.

I came to realize that one experience was worth a hundred theories. I perceived that the way of philosophy and psychology did not produce Christlike men and women. I was seeking truth, and none of these studies seemed to bring me close to reality.

About this time I was unconsciously beginning to take steps toward God, because I was starting to realize my limitations. The first step was when I realized I could not change people. Who was I to judge? We make molds for others because we think we are standards by which their thinking and acting should be judged. Our intolerance is rooted in our conceit.

My next step was when I attained an intellectual appreciation of humility. This came to me in reading George Washington's letters to Congress, and I saw the beauty of that rare combination of courage and humility. Before this I had looked upon humility as the opposite of courage, and had regarded it as a weakness.

My next step was when I realized I had been born wanting, that is, selfish. I have never known a "wholesome" small child who spent his days in thinking what he could do for his mother and father!

It seems to me that conceit and selfishness are about the two most devastating traits we can have, and it was a shock to me to find myself convicted of both of them.

Then I realized that my occasional periods of depression were the reaction from periods of overconfidence. In spite of my efforts toward an "esthetic equilibrium," these periods of overconfidence persisted. I found that overconfidence and the subsequent depression were contagious, and I could not find a serum that would make me immune.

My next step was in realizing that if all stood on their rights, we would have a state of anarchy. I thus found out for myself the truth of one of the fundamental principles of Jesus' teachings.

Most of us make excuses for our sins—we explain them to ourselves intellectually, and we are apt to be tolerant of similar sins in others. We are, however, intolerant of other kinds of sins—ones we have not committed or had the temptation to commit. We fight against facing ourselves. I had achieved some honesty with myself, when I realized, with a shock, that I had been really only making intellectual excursions, and that I did not have a real desire to be spiritual.

At times I seemed worse than the world, and at times the world seemed even worse than I. I could see that men who thought they were good really were not so; and were what the world calls good only because they were cowards, afraid of others' opinions, or were afraid of consequences.

I saw men and women who thought they were good completely bowled over by sin when their needs or even wants were frustrated. There were others who were restless and confused, and who did not understand their own restlessness and confusion. They judged one another largely by the physical shell in which the soul was encased. Sometimes they were so deeply rooted in conceit that they disliked even constructive criticism. "Sensitiveness" is often unbounded egotism. They disliked anyone who made them face themselves. I saw many men and women keeping themselves active in one way or another so that they would not have to face themselves. Some were trying to obtain a temporary oblivion. Sometimes they were trying to obtain peace through physical exhaustion.

During my search for truth I studied some of the so-called "new thought" books, but I came to realize that these were very old. They were all variations, with new vocabularies, of "mental science"—belief in one's own powers, although one's own powers were often called God!

About this time I was confronted with various calamities and problems. I have never believed that the God who loves us would want us to suffer, but undoubtedly his love is wise enough to allow us to suffer if it is necessary for us to do so in order that we shall find him. There is nothing "mushy" about the love of God. If you have a cancer he does not give you a soothing syrup. It looked as though the results of my life's work were going to be lost. Figuratively, I had been living on the sixtieth floor, and God mercifully allowed me to fall out the window. It looked as though my little world was breaking up. I developed more than an intellectual understanding of humility; I developed a feeling of humility. What a difference between that which we know in our head and that which we know in our heart!

I realized that my life had been built on sand, and forgetting my futile efforts to change others, I started in with all my will power to change myself. I had a God-given wish to be different from what I was. I used all the intellectual methods, the methods of reasoning. I tried to eliminate sin by dealing with one sin at a time. The trouble with this was that while I was working on sin number two, sin number one started coming back. I tried new interests. I tried "neglecting" my sins. Finally I realized I could not change myself, and as I did not like myself as I was, I was trapped.

In despair I turned to the Church. I am a church member, and as a boy I had attended church and Sunday School regularly, but because of my memories, I returned to it reluctantly.

My wife and I are now enthusiastic church workers, but I had gone to church very little since I was a boy. For that reason perhaps I can look at it more objectively than those who have been churchmen always. I have to admit that during my early church association I learned nothing; I was bored and depressed by its solemnity; and I found no "glad tidings."

One clergyman tried to arouse my emotions, although it seemed to me my emotions were sufficiently aroused. Besides, although finding God may be a very emotional experience, I do not see how one can find God through one's emotions. Another told me to go to the house of God, and that I would find God there. I had often sat alone in churches and cathedrals, but had not found him. Since then I have talked to people who have found God in church, but I have also talked to people who found him in bar rooms. Another talked to me in theological and figurative language that I could not understand. Another talked to me in frightening language and gave me more than I could bear. I was very unhappy, but it seemed like jumping from the frying pan into the fire to "offer myself as a burnt offering" and become "broken bread and spilled wine."

I felt that there was an available power somewhere, but I did not know how to avail myself of it. I felt as Emerson did when he was searching for God: "I wish to know the laws of this wonderful power, that I may domesticate it . . . that I may learn to live with it wisely, court its aid, catch sight of its splendor, feel its approach, hear and save its oracles and obey them."

The first good advice coming to me was from a

layman. He advised me to study the life and teach-ings of Jesus Christ. Dr. Henry Drummond was helpful. In his book, *The Changed Life*, he explains that we tend to become like those we admire, and that as we hold the mirror up to our Lord we tend to become, or want to become, like him.

I believed in God, but I wanted a fulfillment of the promise that I could find him and know he was God. I wanted him to make himself known to me, to reveal himself to me. I wanted his guidance and the power to overcome.

I instinctively knew there were conditions I must fulfill, but I could not find anyone to tell me what they were.

It seemed to me that I was at a confusing impasse. I was told I would find God when I followed his commandments—loved him and loved my neighbor; but I could not do these things.

However, God kept his promise as he always does. I was searching for him with all my heart, and he put various books in my hand and revealed certain things to me that cleared the situation for me.

It was a great relief to me when I found that the only condition required of me was willingness. I learned that I need only be willing to be obedient. I learned that if I was willing, he would give me the power to obey him, he would fight my battles for me.

It took me a few days to understand the meaning of self-surrender, and let me frankly admit that I shrank from it even though I had been seeking God for years. It meant the giving up of my will, and I had always been very self-willed. Instinctively, I felt that when the demon of self-will leaves a man, "it teareth him." It meant giving up all my own objectives and planning. It means surrendering all my opinions to him for correction. It meant being willing to surrender everybody and everything. It meant taking up my cross, allowing self-will to be crucified, and following wherever God led me.

If people had in their hearts that which is in their head and on their lips there would be conversions every time the Lord's Prayer is spoken. "Thy will be done" means the giving ourselves to him. The will is the man, and if we really surrender our will we surrender ourselves.

Many want to know what God is going to ask them to do before they agree to do it, but he will not tell them. They must trust his love. The surrender must be an absolute surrender to obedience, just as it is in enlisting in the army. Even then, he does not lay his whole plan for us before us. He gives us only one step at a time.

The duty of all of us at all times is to increase the area of our surrender. This brings us increasing love, understanding, and power.

Let me give this word of encouragement: I was about the least likely person of anyone I knew whom God would use, yet God has been using me since I found him. I believe he has been doing so because I know I am unworthy and never can be worthy as of myself; and because I have tried to get myself out of the way and let him have possession of me. He says: "My strength is made perfect in weakness."

We must not exult—we must be awed—when he does use us.

Confessions of a Layman

By a Lawyer

UNTIL RECENTLY I assumed myself to be a Christian, but I was wrong. I was brought up according to accepted traditions of decency, attended church regularly, served twenty years as deacon or elder, taught for some years in Sunday School, said grace at the table regularly and read the Scriptures occasionally, tithed both time and money for church and community welfare, supported my family according to American standards of living, and voted regularly. I observed such of the Ten Commandments as are usually observed by decent people, but I violated continuously the First Commandment.

My own parents did not continue their practice of Christianity with anything like the devotion of my grandparents, though they were thoroughly good people and continued as pillars in the church. They relied on their example of good living to teach us children right from wrong. We were not taught the Scriptures or disciplined in God's moral laws except at church.

I in my generation have not comprehended the First Commandment at all, and have not taught its precepts to my children. I was not conscious of any real dependence on God's will or his plan of life for me and for all persons, nor of his love for humanity.

I really never prayed with impartial desire to know and do God's will and to be governed strictly by his laws and love affecting human relations. I never learned whether prayer was practical, or whether it worked. Feeling no great need, of course my prayers had no substance to them that required or justified God's answer. My mind was not open to the inner voice or the prompting of the Spirit. I conducted my life from day to day by self-will and by the advice of my fellow men. Not God's plan for my life but my own plans and purposes and those of the groups to whom I owed loyalty absorbed my thought. To those who understand the relationship to the Spiritual Father of mankind as it should be, my life must have appeared like that of any other self-centered, undisciplined child of a natural parent.

It is strange, too, now that I look back over a period of years, that my ministers have been, without exception, good men. They argued, sometimes with great conviction, God's case. Yet they never bore witness to his working so that I could see it and be led to apply it for myself. They talked to me as a part of a congregation; God was abstract, not personal. I had faith that my minister was a Christian but what he said was something to be enjoyed or rejected as an intellectual experience of the moment. It did not change my life or any life that I know of into that of a practicing, praying Christian.

At no meeting of my fellow deacons or elders in more than ten years was there ever any testimony offered to the working of God's will or the answering of prayers among them. In fact, we never prayed. The minister did that on all occasions. So far as was revealed at any meeting, none of us ever prayed. It was not even assumed that we did. Our meetings were for the business of the church and, as such, deadly dull. Yet we thought of ourselves as functioning Christians.

I believe a clear majority in my town assumes itself to be Christian. Yet we do not hear God mentioned, as being vital, in conversation, correspondence, press, business, politics, or schools. In college, religion is a small and generally regarded unimportant subject.

I have not been guilty of the ordinary crimes mentioned in the Ten Commandments but I sent all my children to schools and colleges where the Ten Commandments were merely points of view, matters for man-made judgment and experience. Their minds were trained in secular materials so they might be sharp enough to decide what is right and wrong for themselves. Yet in chemistry, physics, biology, and in all the natural sciences there were absolute laws that they were disciplined not to ignore. On the other hand they were abandoned to learn at bitter cost, without warning, that the laws governing the moral conduct of persons are also absolute, and their violation more devastating than the violation of the laws of things. For this and many other sins like it, I ask God's forgiveness.

Recently I asked laymen in other cities and other denominations if their experience was like mine. They agreed it was. Some added, however, what I believe to be true, that in nearly every community there are a few men and women who do practice Christianity and find that prayer works in their lives.

But they are too timid to make themselves known, and the rest of us have not been eager enough to find and learn from them. They lack a certain missionary spirit which they would have if they only knew how desperately the rest of us need their witness. We need to know of their experience, their assurance, their teaching, to strengthen our faith so that we, too, may accept the truth.

About a year ago I began to meet men who, like me, had been fooling themselves; we were all untaught and without wisdom in spiritual affairs. We were groping for the faith that we knew our forefathers had, that was a part of the American way of life, that gave men convictions they were willing to sacrifice for. We felt frustrated and weary in selfpursuits, and tired for lack of hope and purpose. Finally we began to search out men who were definitely relying upon the Spirit of God for guidance. We found them. That God works and that prayers were answered was revealed to us beyond a doubt by laymen like ourselves. In spite of the old habits of mind and the reserves of nature, we had faith in what we heard and saw. We began feebly to use prayer in our own lives. We began at the same time, and as a result of prayer, to be conscious of our sins, sins we never recognized before. And as we became conscious of them we began to feel the need for more prayer and meditation and guidance from God. For, to be Christian, apparently we must feel a need. As long as we are self-sufficient we do not need God and will not pray. And therefore we will not be Christian, whatever else we may do that is good.

Without prayer I find it impossible to get rid of

my personal bias, the confusion and the clamor and the tensions that come from pursuing my own will. With it I find release, impartiality, greater endurance, hope of the future, and a joy in living that seems in tune with the nature of things.

At present I find myself practicing the presence of God for very short periods. Even so, I am able at last to think of God as a Spirit that can be comprehended in prayer and meditation. That concept remains and is good in my relations with other men, far beyond the short periods of its conscious retention in my mind. With practice and with deliberate reading and fellowship and the exercise of the will (a very manly pursuit, by the way), more perfection is assured. I am beginning at last to comprehend what practicing Christianity really means.

III

The Layman in His Church

The Church and Its Laymen

James E. Kavanagh

WHAT IS THE CHURCH'S CHALLENGE to the layman? I do not know. For sixty years or more I have been a regular attendant at church services of various denominations. So far, I have not met with any particular challenge in all those years, other than that I attend church services, make contributions toward the suport of the church and its various benevolences, act as a trustee, help on committee work, aid as a Sunday School teacher, take up collection, or act as an usher.

Those duties I have performed from time to time, and as a result have come to be regarded as a rather good layman.

However, for many years I have felt that the Church was not demanding enough from its laymen. The churches seem to me to be run and managed by preachers and priests, professional men highly trained, and specifically educated for the task.

These professional men are looked upon by the average layman as being rather sacred—superior—and generally have been placed on pedestals above the rank and file of the congregation. If the preacher has a big congregation to whom he can preach, he is generally regarded as a success. But is he a success?

It seems to me that the challenge to the laymen has not yet been issued; if so, it is a very feeble challenge and one that is too easily met. My further conviction is that when it is made it must be made by the clergy.

If, therefore, what I say seems to be directed more toward the clergy than the laymen, it is because I believe there is a challenge to the clergy that must first be met.

Let me preface any remarks by stating that I owe a debt of gratitude to the Church and the clergy which I can never repay. I have listened with great profit to ministers of various denominations on an average of well over once a Sunday for over sixty years. If any of my remarks seem to be critical, they are made with only one thought in my mind, and that is to expose some of the thoughts that frequently cross my mind as I have longed for a more vigorous and successful presentation of the Christian way of life.

I sometimes wonder just what many preachers are seeking to do? Are they trying to make the teachings of Christ more difficult to understand and follow? Is there so much mystery about the Christian religion? Is it difficult to understand? Does the pastor desire his people to be brave, generous, kind, truthful, unselfish, industrious, and considerate of the rights of others? Are those not the teachings of Christ, spoken as they were, in simple words, easily understood, and devoid of argument?

Has the Protestant Church unconsciously built up a ritual which consists of Bible reading, congregational singing, prayers, announcements, and a sermon? The order is so fixed in most churches that one could stay at home and by the clock be able to tell just when the sermon is to begin. Does this cut-and-dried systematic procedure of worship not approach a ritual? Does it not tend to make many people think that God can be worshiped only in this way? Shouldn't the congregation be treated to illustrations of current successful Christian living? Can't sermons be taken from the village or city life? Must they all be taken from the Bible? Why should not laymen and laywomen assist more in the religious services of the church? Is it an implication that they are not good enough? Is it only ordained men or ministers who should read the Bible or our hymns to a congregation? Many hymns are not understood by the congregation. Some hymns are of praise, others are prayers. Would it not be well to have some laymen read and explain them so that the people may know them better and realize whether they are praying or praising when they sing? Not many persons in a congregation would make the statements they so cheerfully and often blindly make as they sing our church hymns. That is, they would lack the courage to make them in private conversation if they really knew what they meant.

In the course of a week I should suppose a pastor could secure from his parish, or the daily press or radio, events which would well illustrate the Christian religion in action. That is what the Christian religion is for. Its claim is that it can soothe sorrow, strengthen souls, guide people into ways of life which produce a sense of well-being. Why go back to the Bible characters for all or most of our illustrations?

If the highly paid executives of big business hold their positions through their ability to organize men

and women into systematic ways of life, why should
not the men who are especially trained as leaders in
our churches do the same? What is the biggest business in this land? Is it banking, railroading, insurance, merchandise, transporting or manufacturing
goods? Or is it teaching men and women how to live?
That is the biggest job any man can tackle. I saw
fifteen young men graduate from a theological semi-
nary a few weeks ago. As I watched them, I couldn't
help but admire them, their courage, their lack of
personal ambition, going out into the world to
operate on the most difficult of all objects, the human
will, or mind, or spirit. Surely they were stepping
into big business. Did they know it? I wonder!

In some respects the business of the Church may
be compared to big business. Is it not perfectly
proper to state that the Christian religion needs to be
"sold" to the public? I think it is. I also think that
methods akin to those adopted by business houses
should and could be adopted to "sell" the teachings
of our Master to selfish man, who is largely dominated by his animal instincts.

Yes, I think if Christianity is to become the big
business of the world it should seek to adopt some
practices of business. The young clergyman might
well be given a course in the management of men
in addition to a course in the winning of souls, so
that he will go into his new duties, not as a novice,
but more or less a seasoned, sure master of his calling.

"Good goods properly shown will sell themselves."
This is a well-known business slogan. Are the
"goods" or "services" that the Church has to offer
"good"? If so are they properly shown?

Testimonials are sought out constantly by manufacturers and distributors. These testimonials are paraded before the public as evidence of the superiority of the particular service or commodity.

We all know how proud the big business house is of its satisfied customers. Has the Church a lot of satisfied customers? Or have its customers been disappointed? If they are satisfied why not have them "tell the world"?

Personally, I have been connected with the "selling" end of a life insurance company all my business life. When I began I was sent out as a solicitor. Yes, that's the word, "solicitor" — begging, asking for favors, asking people to buy, to part with their money; talking, arguing, and getting nowhere, but feeling much like a panhandler or a mendicant. No wonder I gave up after a few days. Fortunately for me I was gotten in again and given a vision of the good that life insurance does. I was taught to think, not of what I was going to get in the way of commission, but of what prospects themselves could do if they would but hire the services of a life insurance company—how they could systematically save for the future and provide for their dependents or themselves in old age. Then I felt like Santa Claus. I acquired the "giving away" Santa Claus spirit. I was always "giving away," giving people a chance to make their lives better.

Now isn't that something like the job of the clergyman? He does not need to beg or to be a panhandler. He is a doer of good, a dispenser of largesse. As such he soon would acquire a feeling of certainty about his job. A man breathes confidence in himself and his goods and services (if he really has that confidence); and if at the same time he has a technique of doing what he wants done or of getting others to do it for him, he is sure to succeed. That's the trick! That's the challenge! The clergy is challenged to challenge the layman. Get the church's activities out of one man's hands into the hands of many. Multiply, expand, grow.

When that passage in the Bible which reads "Where two or three are gathered together . . ." is used to cover up failure, it is a mistake. It is much better to have two or three thousand gathered together. Success cannot be achieved by a church that is operated by one man. Give the laymen those "dividends of satisfaction" that come from doing good.

"Give the ball" to the layman. Make the church into a "meeting place." Give them more specific things to do. Make performers of the people. Their actions will speak louder than their words.

The Christian religion is a live thing. It is like electricity, it transforms the recipient. It stimulates him. It makes him want to do good. All of this activity implies the necessity for spiritual resouces which, for the most part, we laymen do not possess. The clergy must recognize that we and they have failed in sufficiently building ourselves up along this line. With the calls for a larger share in the program of the Church, we laymen must realize the need for spiritual preparation. And the Church must gather us into groups according to our needs and give us the training we have so far greatly neglected.

God Is Man's Crying Need

John D. Rockefeller, Jr.

IN THE YEAR 1883 a boy of nine and his three sisters were baptized in the Euclid Avenue Baptist Church, Cleveland, Ohio. Their parents were earnest, Christian people; both had been active in church and Sunday School work all their lives.

In their home, family prayers before breakfast had always been the custom, each one taking part, either reading from the Bible in turn or reciting a verse of Scripture, many of which were thus learned and vividly retained throughout life. The blessing was asked before each meal. On Sunday the parents and children went together to church and Sunday School. The father was superintendent of the school; the mother, superintendent of the primary department; the children, as they grew older, often acted as supply teachers. Friday night was prayer-meeting night; the whole family always attended the meeting. At an early age the children were encouraged by their mother to take part like the older people, either in a brief prayer or a word of personal experience.

Sunday was invariably observed as a day of rest; only necessary duties were performed. A cold dinner was the rule, that work might be reduced to a minimum. No studying was allowed or games of any kind, while the reading of the Bible and Sunday books only was permitted. If the children had done wrong during the week, their mother would point out to them earnestly how in so doing they had sinned against God, whose forgiveness she would lead them to seek in prayer. The day was a happy day, for it was a family day.

Business soon made it necessary for the father to be in New York during the winter months. Therefore, from the time the youngest of them was hardly more than a baby, the entire family migrated each fall to New York, and for some years spent the winters there, returning to Cleveland for the summers. It was thus that the Fifth Avenue Baptist Church became ultimately its adopted home, and the children members of the Sunday School.

The son was a diffident boy and ill at ease among strangers. To make it easier for him to join the new Sunday School, his mother formed about him a class of boys of his own age and she herself became its teacher. This class grew to be an institution of the church. As one group of boys grew up and went away to school or college, another took its place. Thus for years this devoted Christian mother shared with an ever-widening circle the brooding love, the wise guidance, and the Christlike spirit which throughout her life had so profound an influence on her son.

Is it any wonder then that in later years he reverently erected the tower of the Riverside Church to her memory and put in it the carillon, that on the wings of its far-flung tones the inspiration of her love for God and her fellow men, her dauntless courage, and her radiant faith might be carried to the uttermost parts of the earth?

During the years of his college life, spent away from home, this diffident youth allied himself at the outset with a local church as a regular attendant and shortly became the teacher of a class of boys in its Sunday School; this position he occupied for several years.

After graduation from college, on his return to New York, it was natural that this young man should go at once into the Young Men's Bible Class. Thus it was that, in the early fall of '97, he joined the class of which Mr. Charles E. Hughes was the stimulating and inspiring leader. The world knows him today as an outstanding public servant, a great statesman, and a distinguished Chief Justice of the Supreme Court. As illustrative of his keen sense of humor and reminiscent of the many stories he told with such gusto, may I digress a moment to relate an incident that occurred perhaps a dozen years ago.

It took place at a summer resort in the White Mountains. Judge and Mrs. Hughes were lunching with some friends who asked Mrs. Rockefeller and me to join them on the piazza of their cottage after lunch. As we were chatting together, the Judge told his friends that for some years he had been a trustee of the Rockefeller Foundation, that he had greatly enjoyed the association and had given his best thought to the problems that confronted the Board, but that upon reaching a certain age he had been courteously given to understand that he had passed the period of usefulness, shortly after which time he was retired. "Whereupon, the next year," the Judge added, "I was made Chief Justice of the Supreme **Court.**"

This was the great personality whose place, as leader of the class, the retiring young man, the identity of whom you have already guessed, was ultimately to take.

Upon Mr. Hughes' resignation in the fall of '99, I acted from time to time as a supply leader until the end of May, 1900. That fall full leadership was conferred upon me, although having sat for two years at the feet of this brilliant mind and fine spirit, I was deeply conscious of my inability to be in any adequate sense his successor.

The eight years of my leadership, which ended in the fall of 1907, were among the richest and most rewarding years of my life. As my father once said: "The leadership of the class is a great thing for John, but pretty hard on the boys."

It is because I covet for every young man the opportunities which association with this men's class brought me, as well as because I am so grateful for the home life and training which led up to my connection with it, that I have ventured to speak thus intimately and at such length of my early life. Against such a background, duty, service, sacrifice were subjects of constant consideration; the dedication of one's life to them, under God's impelling love and inspiration of Christ's life, an ideal ever to be striven for.

I wonder how many of us who are parents talk to our children of duty, of service, of sacrifice. I wonder how many young people give these lofty ideals more than a passing thought. And yet they are as vital today to the development of character as they always have been.

In speaking at a parent-teachers' meeting at the Lincoln School many years ago, I said that I could see nothing in the modern school curriculum that took the place of the wood pile and the cow in my father's early training. It can hardly be supposed that he got up at five o'clock to milk the cow before starting for school or kept the family wood pile stocked because of his inordinate fondness for those occupations. Rather were they necessary functions of home life, the daily performance of which fell to his lot, as did other tasks to the other children. Having thus to render currently a service vital to the well-being of the family developed in him the power to make himself do the duty that presented itself wholly apart from how he felt about it—a power that was surely the foundation for that complete self-mastery which was one of the outstanding characteristics of his life.

But while it is regrettably true that duty, service, and sacrifice are too often relegated to the past with hoop skirts, stocks, and wigs, among the young men and women who were in the armed forces and behind the lines, be it said to their everlasting credit, that there were countless evidences of high allegiance to duty and of spontaneous dedication to service and sacrifice which are beyond praise. Thus it would appear that these latent qualities were developed by the war in unnumbered instances.

Must we conclude, then, that war, with all its ghastly trappings and consequences, is necessary in order to bring out these qualities—qualities which are even more essential to the making and maintaining of a just peace than to the winning of the war?

No, a thousand times no, for to do so would be to belie the belief in God. If we believe in God we must believe that he can use even the horrors of war to accomplish his purposes. In God alone is to be found the power that through the ages has impelled men to the performance of the highest duty, has inspired them to the most unselfish service, has given them strength to make the greatest sacrifices.

Hitler, Mussolini, Tojo have sought to substitute belief in the State for belief in God. Utterly have they failed. Instead, they developed in millions of their followers a fanatical zeal which, glorying in might, committed to destruction, utterly devoid of justice and mercy, resulted in a return to the barbarism of the savages. There is no power other than the power of God, working often in mysterious ways, no faith except faith in him and in his eternal purposes that can turn man from destructive ends to constructive ends, from selfishness to service. Never did the world need that power, that faith, more than today.

Faith in that creative force which we call God, a return to the simple, courageous faith in him which animated the founders and builders of this nation, the cultivation of their rugged spiritual qualities, their stern sense of duty and willingness to sacrifice, and a rekindling of the deep, impelling belief in God which they had are the crying need of a broken and suffering world.

The home, the church, the Sunday School are the custodians of that faith—the institutions upon which rests the responsibility for its preservation and its propagation. While they have often fallen short in the discharge of their sacred duty, it is nevertheless true that the future of civilization depends upon the earnestness with which they reorganize their plans and methods and the sincerity with which they make the living as well as the teaching of God's love and Christ's life, their greatest concern. To that end, the Bible, the greatest book of all ages, must be restored to its rightful place, for in its diligent study is to be found the way of life.

To that end, businessmen—all of us must play out part, for in the last analysis we are the home, the Church, and the Sunday School, and they will be no better than we are—are determined, with God's help, to work. The process of revitalizing the spiritual forces of the world must begin in our own lives.

The Church and Our Responsibility

HAROLD S. MINER

IT HAS ALWAYS SEEMED TO ME that the recognition of mutual responsibilities is the keystone of successful co-operative effort. Applying this rule to the development of the Christian Church, it may be helpful if we try to define and outline some of the more obvious responsibilities as between church and chuchman.

As a layman, what have I a right to expect of my church? And what has my chuch a right to expect of me?

In every organization there is apt to develop a tendency to allow purely operational functions to supplant, rather than supplement, primary objectives. So, in a church, it is easy to lose, in a welter of administrative detail, its principal purpose, which is to help us discover and do the will of God in our everyday lives. There is a dangerous tendency in our modern culture to emphasize quantity at the expense of quality. The progress of a church is too often measured by attendance figures and by the size and variety of its organizations. Yet, every businessman learns that it is not the volume of sales but the net profit which spells success for his undertaking. So, too, God does not take inventory of possessions; God counts hearts. As a layman, I believe I have a right to expect that my church will recognize this truth, and that it will appraise its accomplishments in terms of net spiritual profit.

Too many churches of today have found it necessary or politic to confine their teachings to chicken-hearted generalities. For my part, I do not want my pastor to sugar-coat his preaching of the gospel. If I cannot hear the truth, and be the better for having heard it, it should be evident to me that my search for Christian knowledge is no more sincere than was that of the Pharisees when they questioned the statement of Jesus that the truth would make them free. Jesus said, "If I say the truth why do you not believe me? He that is of God heareth God's words! Ye therefore hear them not because ye are not of God." Whereupon the Pharisees took up stones to cast at him. Well, nowadays we do not throw stones, but we do sometimes plug up our ears, go away and sulk, or just stay at home. I believe I have a right to expect that my church will constantly keep me aware of my Christian obligations by teaching God's law for human conduct with fearless and aggressive persistence.

What does my chuch have a right to expect of me? First, and above all else, my church has a right to expect that I will so conduct my personal life and affairs as to indicate the honesty of my profession of faith in Jesus Chrst. There is no greater obstacle to church progress than a church member who lives in such a way as to justify others in pointing the finger of scorn at his church because of his manner of living, and the more prominent the so-called churchman, the greater the harm.

Our church has a right to expect us to do our share of the church work. I think we will all agree that we cannot buy immunity from our own obligations to our church by hiring a minister, be he ever so capable. We must bear our part of the load. To some, this involves organizational duties, but to every last one of us it means the providing of financial support and the fostering of a spirit of affection and encouragement toward one another.

My church has the right to expect me to acknowledge myself openly as a Christian churchman. This may require courage. The devil's greatest triumph is a popular acceptance of the idea that Christian character is "soft," and how we hate to be called "soft"! But can we read the history of how our Christian saints and martyrs throughout the ages stood up under torment and persecution, and still believe their faith was "soft"? Can we contemplate Christ's road to the Cross and still call Christian character "soft"?

Isn't it a fact that it is not Christian character that is soft, but we, who call ourselves Christians, are becoming "soft" because we are more concerned with popularity than personal integrity? There is a type of courage which transcends physical courage. It is the kind of courage required today to smile at the skeptics, to ignore the scornful, and to keep right on trying to be a Christian. Christ recognized this type of courage when he said, "Blessed are ye when men shall revile you and persecute you and shall say all manner of evil against you falsely, for my sake. Rejoice, and be exceeding glad! For great is your reward in heaven! For so persecuted they the prophets which were before you!"

My church has a right to expect me to practice positive as well as negative Christianity. It is not enough that I shall not steal; I shall not kill; I shall not bear false witness. A noted English preacher expressed this thought beautifully when he said: "Christianity does not consist in abstaining from doing things no gentleman would think of doing, but consists of doing things that are unlikely to occur to anyone who is not in touch with the spirit of Christ" (Robert H. W. Shepherd). What a world of meaning is crammed into those few words: "doing things that are unlikely to occur to anyone who is not in touch with the spirit of Christ."

Against the war's smouldering background of insecurity and fear, the shadows of life stood out in unusually bold relief. From our altars of every faith we heard pleas for strength to bear our losses—prayers seldom heard in prewar years. But strength is not a quality induced by idleness, no matter what sins are not committed. Strength results from action. Our Christian heritage, like the heritage of liberty, demands that we be eternally vigilant, positive, alert. Jesus was never negative. His great command to his disciples was that they carry the gospel to every corner of the earth. Evangelism is positive. Subtract evangelism from the Christian Church and all you have left is a lifeless society. My church has the right to expect me to be alert at all times to challenge any feeling of complacency the church may develop and to keep insisting that it shall recognize the overwhelming obligation and tremendous opportunity inherent in our critical world situation today.

To live up to the obligations which my church imposes on me, I must try harder than ever before to be a Christian, in word and deed, in my own personal relationships. If each of us would make such an effort today, what vast power would be generated! There is no magic formula for group power. It is just simple arithmetic. When two out of ten exert power, the group is 20 per cent effective; when ten out of ten exert power, the group is 100 per cent effective. We cannot escape our obligations as Christian churchmen by neglecting or running away from our church. It would be like trying to escape from ourselves. And any man who wants to escape because he can discover nothing worth while in the collective experience of a group of believers (which we call "the church") will certainly find nothing but delusion and emptiness within his own solitary self. This I know: God's purpose for us is not that we shall escape! It is that we shall try, and keep on trying, in the face of every discouragement. Until this eternal truth is understood and accepted by all, sedatives, anesthetics, and complicated programs of man-made guidance will continue to usurp the throne of faith in the minds and hearts of men. I believe with all my soul that when we have conquered men's instinctive desire to escape we have taken the first step down a road to new usefulness and happiness. What has our church a right to expect of us? That as Christian laymen we will try to find our part and exert our strength in building Christian character into the everyday life of the world. May God grant us the will, the understanding, and the fortitude to succeed.

Christianity Outside the Church

FREDERICK C. SHIPLEY

A LAYMAN SOMETIMES FEELS that he is unimportant in a church unless he is an officer or at least a member of a committee. He should remember that a church without laymen would scarcely be a church at all. The work of a church reaches fruition only when the Christian ideals which it teaches are put into practice outside the church by its laymen in everyday life.

I have said "outside of the church" because I do not here refer to the work which a layman does within the church itself. Work done for the church as an organization, our contributions both in money and effort, our service on committees, our assistance in special functions—all these are important, but there is something needed beyond. A church cannot long exist just for itself alone.

And I have said "in everyday life" because I do not here refer to those rather special tasks which a Christian layman undertakes outside of the church. Service for a charity or a welfare organization, participation in or contributions to a drive for a community chest, for the Red Cross, or even for war bonds—all of these things are important also, but there is something needed beyond.

What I particularly refer to here are those acts of everyday Christianity, not of an organized sort, not

of the kind that attracts attention, not of the kind
that even has a name, but those things which form
" . . . that best portion of a good man's life, his little,
nameless, unremembered acts of kindness and of
love."

These often are the hardest. They are not spec-
tacular. We cannot boast of them, even to ourselves.
And these tasks are never ended; we must be forever
at them, weekdays as well as Sundays, fifty-two weeks
a year, throughout a lifetime. And the necessity for
this sort of Christian action extends into every nook
and cranny of our lives, even into our thoughts.

Sometimes thinking is the hardest of all. The
Golden Rule is a simple rule to state; but even to
know its application is not always easy. Too often
doing for others as we would have others do unto
us becomes merely doing to others what we expect
others to do to us, and that is mere tit for tat, mere
retaliation. That is not the Golden Rule, but the old
law—an eye for an eye and a tooth for a tooth. The
hardest thing in all the Christian code is to understand, when someone seems to have done us an injury, why he did it. It is easy to retaliate, when we
have been hurt. It is very hard indeed to stop and try
to understand—to see the thing the way the other
person sees it; to see, perhaps, that he never intended
us an injury at all, but acted thoughtlessly, or more
probably in imagined self-defense.

A peacemaker is not always the person who merely
turns the other cheek. Even turning the other cheek
is sometimes easier than the kind of thinking which
is necessary to make an enemy not want to hit us—
in a word, leading him to understand us by demon-

strating that we have taken the trouble to understand him.

There are very few disputes which do not involve misunderstanding on one side or the other, and frequently on both. At the present moment we are in the midst of an epidemic of labor disputes—strikes. We well enough know the pattern: a period of refusal to understand, with industry tied up and men out of work, and then after days, or even weeks, the warring sides give in, to search for a common ground; and eventually an agreement is reached. Why only eventually? Who does the long period of misunderstanding so often have to come first?

A critic has said that every tragedy that was ever written has as its basis a misunderstanding. Hamlet misunderstood his own mother and ended by misunderstanding himself. Othello strangled Desdemona, whom he loved more than all the world, because he misunderstood, not only her, but his own loyal friends who tried to get him to understand before it was too late. The stock line of drama is, "But you don't understand," to which the answer is, "I understand perfectly. Goodbye." Trite as this situation is, it will remain universal in the representation of human life as long as the failing which it portrays remains so deeply seated.

A deeper, more genuine understanding of our fellow men lies at the center of the second great commandment in Jesus' teaching. One of the best ways to show ourselves Christians—no, not show ourselves but *be* Christians—is to practice this understanding of our fellow men throughout the week, throughout the year. Our lives will be the richer for it.

IV

The Layman in His Business Life

Bridging the Gap

John G. Ramsay

ON A TRAIN RECENTLY my thoughts were interrupted by a commotion in the front of the car. The conductor was reprimanding a Negro who had sat down in a seat alone. The back of the seat in front of him had been reversed, and the "Railroad Brotherhood" conductor said, "Who do you think you are, taking up all this space?" The Negro man quietly replied, "This was the only vacant seat in the car and I could not reverse the seat in front of me." The conductor gave a vigorous heave and the stubborn seat would not budge. With the aid of others, including the Negro, the seat was reversed.

The train stopped at a station and the conductor hurried through the car. As he passed I heard two men remark: "Good stuff, conductor, these niggers must be kept in their place."

Passengers were coming into the car and, finding no single seats, began to double up. A Negro sat next to me. He took a manuscript out of his pocket and began to read. I noticed the word "Isaiah" written on the top of the first page. When he finished reading, I said to him, "Are you a preacher?" "Yes, sir, I was just reading my sermon for this morning," was his reply.

"I also have a message to give this morning," I told him. "The topic is, 'How to Bridge the Gap be-

133

tween Religion and Economic Life.' What do you
have to say on that subject?"

"Well, sir, I would say the only way it can be done
is to do what Jesus would do, regardless of what
others do." I became so engrossed in our conversation that I passed my station, without realizing it.

At the next station I took a taxi. Beginning a conversation with the taxi driver, I asked him how to
bridge the gap between religion and economic life.
"It can't be done," he replied. I spent the rest of the
trip convincing him it could be done and as we
reached my destination and I was leaving the cab,
he said, "Well, sir, I still say it can't be done, but by
God, we gotta do it."

It is good that we realize and acknowledge that
there are gaps to be bridged. How are we to bridge
them? Perhaps the advice of the Negro minister is a
good place to begin: do what Jesus would do.

That is a challenge that came to me as a young man
when reading *In His Steps,* by Charles M. Sheldon.
To help me to understand better what Jesus would
do my wife bought me a red-letter Testament, which
I have continued to study.

It is necessary that we have an understanding of
what we mean by the word "religion." My dictionary
says: "Religion, a belief binding the spiritual nature
of man to a supernatural being." We have accepted
this definition and therefore have not found it hard
to separate the spiritual man from the material or
economic man.

Jesus is different. He demands the whole. "Thou
shalt love the Lord thy God with all thy heart, and
with all thy soul, and with all thy mind. This is the

first and great commandment. And the second is like unto it. Thou shalt love thy neighbor as thyself" (Matthew 22:37-40).

And yet, in the name of the Christian religion, a "believer" in Virginia encourages a snake to bite him. From a news clipping we find the following: "G. L. K. Smith forming 'Christian Veterans.' This is not a call to the weak, not to the vacillating, not to the bootlickers. It is a call to the understanding Christian American veteran, who is tired of being kicked around by bureaucrats, smear artists, refugees, alien-minded propagandists, communists, pluguglies, whip-crackers, and other varieties of un-American vermin who infest our beautiful America."

I am concerned about these false, hate-breeding, ambitious preachers. A couple of weeks ago I was able to give a ride to two hitch hikers. They were young men who had been recently discharged from the armed services. Their homes had been in the backwoods of Tennessee and they were on their way to Detroit. Their sister had gone there as a war worker and had found economic abundance. When I told these two young Americans that there were many thousands of unemployed in the Detroit area due to production cutbacks they said, "We are veterans. They promised us jobs and we will get jobs." Are they to become the storm troopers of these demagogic leaders?

We have failed in our Christian mission to bridge the gap between religion and economic life and our failure has given a green light to false prophets.

Jesus said, "Repent ye: for the kingdom of heaven is at hand (Matthew 3:20).

We need to repent of our failures and seek the vision of the Kingdom individually and collectively. There is a new evangelism needed for our time. It is not enough for the individual to have a soul satisfying experience and then not grow to maturity, developing a social conscience that will bring about the spiritual rebirth of a home, a nation, the world.

Jesus said, "The kingdom of heaven is like unto leaven, which a woman took, and hid in three measures of meal, till the whole was leavened" (Matthew 13:33). The individual is the bridge builder that can span the gap that can leaven the whole of society.

Our forefathers came to America seeking freedom to worship according to the dictates of their conscience, and also from the debt prisons seeking freedom from want. These two purposes were not incompatible. Our forebears saw the danger of separation of religion and economic life and, as a constant reminder, inscribed upon our coins, "In God We Trust." We of this generation have separated our economic life by putting our trust in the coin.

There are two definitions of the word "economics": (1) pertains to money matters and wealth; (2) pertains to the means and methods of living well and wisely.

The first is the definition for the worshipers of mammon and the second is the definition for the Christian. My mother used to tell me that the love of money was the root of all evil but that it was also devilish not to have enough of it!

I believe that organized labor has a clear conception of this. If we have thought that the aims of the organized labor movement for a decent economic life for all are ambiguous, it is time for us to check these aims with our Christian conscience and the teachings of Jesus.

We must have compassion and understanding between the "haves" and "have nots" of our economic and religious life. I am not asking for charity; I am asking for brotherhood.

What is our reaction to the man who is down in economic life? Is it compassion or contempt? If we would understand the reasons why many men and their families are suffering economic degradation, I would suggest the reading of these two books: *Freedom Road,* by Fast, and *The Lord Helps Those,* by Fowler.

What is the reaction of the workers toward the rich? Is it of hate or pity? I believe most workers look upon the rich as being the Pharisee who said, "God, I thank thee, that I am not as other men" (Luke 18:11), and as the money changers who were desecrating the temple.

I know how I used to pity the rich man, for did not Jesus say, "Verily I say unto you, that a rich man shall hardly enter into the kingdom of heaven (Matthew 19:22)"? This was after he had told the rich young ruler, "Go and sell that thou hast, and give to the poor. But when the young man heard that saying, he went away sorrowful for he had great possessions."

Then one day the Lord called me to a new task of bridging the gap between organized religion and organized labor. This meant leaving my wife and children for days at a time and often for weeks. I would not be able to take my troubles and share my victories with my wife as I was accustomed to do. I was afraid of the loneliness of a hotel room, a loneliness that had often led men to sinful lives. It was then that I realized that I also had great possessions. Was I "to go away sorrowful?"

I saw that all I had was mine only by the grace of God. I saw Jesus at Gethsemane and I was ashamed. It is indeed a foolish man who fails to realize that what God gives, he can also take away.

If we are to bridge the gap between religion and economic life, we must first bridge the gaps within economic life. No one is secure while one is insecure, for we are all one humanity.

Delivering the Goods

W. H. GOODWIN

SCIENTISTS responsible for the atomic bomb have collaborated in writing a book called, *One World, or None*. Russia agrees with the title, but sharply disagrees with the British-American interpretation of it. If the clash of ideas comes to war, many people think the bomb will make the decision, and if so it will not be "One World" but "None."

The Church remains; it is eternal. But its great need is spiritually awakened laymen, laymen ordained by the Spirit.

"The tongues of fire" that appeared in the upper room on the day of Pentecost "were distributed and rested on each of them"; there were 120 present, all of whom, with the possible exception of eleven or twelve, were laymen, including some women; and "they were all filled with the Holy Spirit, and began to speak as the Spirit gave them utterance." As one body they brought the impact of their new faith in Jesus Christ on the life of the city that had crucified him six weeks before. They passionately proclaimed the triumph of God in a language everybody could understand.

The significance of the day of Pentecost to us laymen is that we are to be the spearheads of any evangelical movement, the "cutting edge of the tool

of evangelism," as someone has called it, clearing
the way for the truth to reach every man. The significance to the clergy is that it is a waste of time and
effort to be preaching conventional sermons to insti-
tutionalized, static, apathetic, inarticulate congrega-
tions. A minister once announced to his congregation
that there would be a meeting of the Board immediately at the close of the service. A man, who was
not a member of the Board, walked in. He was told
it was a meeting only for the Board. "Well," he said,
"I too was bored." Someone has advised preachers
to stop boring if they don't strike oil in twenty minutes, but that may be no reflection on the sermon.

The average layman knows little about theology.
Maybe we need a new form of pulpit approach, something that will stir us emotionally, stab us awake,
prick us to the heart, compel us to cry out, "What
shall we do?"

I once asked a successful preacher what he would
reply to forty or fifty men who might come up to him
at the close of some Sunday service and say, "We feel
we must do something about that sermon of yours;
what would you suggest?" He said, "Goodwin, I
don't know, we already have sixty ushers."

The story is told that Fred Stone of Broadway,
once marooned by a storm on a western tour,
dropped into the Presbyterian manse to have a chat
with the minister. During the conversation he was
converted. He said to the minister, "What shall I do
now?" He was told to tithe his income. Good, he
would do that, but he is reported to have said, "I am
an actor, what else shall I do?" The reply is not

recorded, but I do remember the days when the New York daily press featured long interviews with Fred Stone on the need for a clean theater and when the quite common advice was, "If you want to go to a good wholesome show, go see "Stepping Stones"— Fred and his daughters.

Some years ago, I was attending an executive meeting of what was called "The Men's Church League," and I asked how Fred Stone was getting on. The reply was, "He is losing his spiritual buoyancy." I wanted to know why. One replied, "I am a member of the Evangelistic Committee of the Federated Churches, and I did suggest that Fred Stone be asked to give his testimony on our platform, but the decision was against it." That moved me to challenge the group to call on Fred Stone and apologize, and have him ordained unto the Christian ministry of the stage, with the promise that the combined resources of the Church would be placed behind him. Livingstone in the jungles of Africa would have nothing on Fred Stone in the jungles of Broadway.

St. Paul told the Ephesians that Christ called "some to be apostles, some prophets, some evangelists, and some pastors and teachers"—to equip the laity for the work of ministry; and surely he may interpret that to mean not only the ministry of money, or of ushers, or of wardens, or of elders, but also the ministry of our occupations, our professions, businesses, and crafts.

The 1946 Montreal-Ottawa Conference of the United Church of Canada resolved that "It should be a condition of membership in the church for every man and woman to accept the responsibility of speaking a good word for Jesus Christ at any time, and of answering the question, 'How can I link up the work of my occupation to the winning of the world for Christ?' "

The answer involves us in functional evangelism. The dictionary meanings of the word "function" are "activity proper to anything"; "mode of action, by which it fulfills its purpose"; "employment"; "profession"; "calling."

Many experiments are being made in functional evangelism. An exploratory movement in the Christian ministry of health and healing was publicly begun in Montreal some years ago. At a medical banquet held in Toronto some time ago about eighty physicians and surgeons listened to Dr. Wilder Penfield, the world famous neurologist of Montreal, and Dr. Edward H. Hume, of New York. One of the outgrowths of that banquet was a proposal to form a World Fellowship of Medicine. What a spearhead for a world evangelical movement that could become!

Functional evangelism is the kind that demonstrates the life of Christ, and the principles of his kingdom, in the performance of the functions proper to one's occupation. It is the most far-reaching, penetrating, revolutionary form of evangelism, and the most difficult.

My business in Montreal was the management of two department stores. The first was under the name of "Murphy," the last under the name of "Goodwins." A neighbor rang me up on a Monday morning to say that he had asked his little girl, Betty, what the story was that the preacher had told the Sunday before. She said, "Goodwins and Murphys will follow us all the days of our lives."

When asked where I got my business ideas, I replied "the Bible." I taught a Bible class. In preparation, I would concentrate on the Scripture lesson early in the mornings before going to business, until by Sunday a principle would be released to my understanding. After teaching the principle to the class on Sunday, I would present it to a group of our executives and heads of departments on Monday mornings in store language for testing in the laboratory of our business.

For instance, take a principle of life revealed through the closing words of the eleventh chapter of Hebrews: "Apart from us they shall not be made perfect." Apart from us in the present, the heroes of faith in the past shall not be made perfect.

On the Monday morning following, I passed the principle on to the drivers of our delivery fleet. I called them together and told them the story of a handkerchief. I took them to a factory in Switzerland, and gave them some of the processes in the making of that handkerchief, how it was then packaged with others and put in a case, passed to the truckdriver, taken to the freight shed, put on a freight car and railroaded to the seaboard, put on a ship and unloaded at Montreal, passed through the customs, trucked to the receiving room, opened and put into reserve, taken from the reserve and displayed on the counter, and one day bought by a customer. The sales check is made out, the handkerchief parceled, the package addressed, sent to the delivery room, and then handed to you. "And" said I, "if you fail to deliver that handkerchief to the right address, all that has happened before goes for nothing. You are the last of the runners in a relay race beginning in Switzerland; to you falls the responsibility of putting the finishing touch on that handkerchief, delivering it to the right address."

And so, apart from the laymen, the preacher's work is not complete, for we are running in a relay race that began with Jesus nearly 2,000 years ago. If any of us fails to deliver the message, at our own exclusive point of contact at any time, the Church fails just there and just then.

Stephen Leacock once wrote of a man who flung himself on his horse and rode madly off in all directions. His enthusiasm may have been commendable, but his confusion was inevitable, for he was only one man on one horse.

The churches of the world have millions of members. If all of us, in our daily pursuits, would first think, then speak of how God's laws as lived and interpreted by Jesus Christ can be made the accepted principle by which men live, and then link up the work of our occupations to the winning of the world for Christ, the Church will be going in millions of different directions all at once, without confusion, bringing the creative, redemptive Spirit of God to the release of tensions in millions of separate circumstances—for it is the Spirit, not the fears of even the atomic bomb, that will convince the world of sin, and of righteousness, and of judgment.

What the world needs above all else is Christian culture, which can be achieved only as the Church sends out into their respective areas of life and influence spiritually ordained, scripturally indoctrinated lay members, as ambassadors of Christ, to recover the lost provinces of Christendom, which are the professions, the businesses, the crafts, and all other of the occupations of men and women the world over.

Bringing Life into Focus

MELVIN J. EVANS

ABOUT A YEAR AGO I was asked by a manufacturing company to study their cost system with an idea to its improvement. A very brief survey brought out the fact that the cost system was not the source of the difficulty in this organization. It was slightly antiquated but good enough for the purpose. The real difficulty lay in the fact that the Board of Directors had lost confidence in the general manager, the foremen hated the superintendent, and altogether there was an almost universal lack of confidence among the men responsible for the destiny of the corporation. Situations of this kind are responsible for reduced profits, reduced production, strikes, etc.

This is one recent example of many similar situations which I have observed. Years ago I resolved to encourage an intensive study of the human problems in business. Through the co-operation of the faculty this was instituted in the College of Engineering at the University of Wisconsin about six years ago. A group of students were interested in the work by Professor E. D. Ayres, then professor of electrical engineering, and work was begun on a purely voluntary basis. We soon saw that our industrial difficulty traced directly back to lack of balanced character on the part of the people involved. In other words, an

146

industrial organization is not a collection of buildings, machinery, patents, etc., but a group of people working together for common objectives. If these people are men of wisdom, a great company inevitably results; if they are petty chiselers, the opposite effect must be expected.

We, therefore, concentrated on the development of techniques which the individual could use to create this balanced personality and character.

As a result of a trip to Europe we came to the conclusion that this same lack of balance in individuals is also at the bottom of our international difficulty. Furthermore, it is difficult to build character in one plant in any one city if opposite conditions prevail in another plant in the same city. Trouble and discord is very much like a disease—it spreads from one focal point to many others. The innocent suffer along with the guilty. Therefore, we are facing a community, a national, and ultimately an international problem if we expect to have international peace.

The predicament in which the world finds itself is due to our failure to distinguish between the laws for things and the laws for men. We have failed to distinguish between knowledge and wisdom. Civilization today is possessed of greater knowledge than all previous centuries combined, but we are sadly short on wisdom.

What would we think of a manufacturer who, faced with the problem of designing a great bomber, called a mass meeting of citizens and indulged in weeks and months of oratory, followed by solemn resolutions that the bomber should possess great speed and power and should be able to carry vast loads of explosives. After a few months of interesting debates, their meetings would probably be terminated by the bombs of a realistic enemy.

When a manufacturer has a design job to do, he immediately secures a staff of engineers skilled in the laws of things, and they follow these laws until success is achieved.

If the bombers are built according to the laws of aero-dynamics and have the proper factors of safety derived from careful experience and tests, the designer has perfect confidence in the result. He doesn't make ecstatic speeches to the engines, exhorting each one to do its best for the flag. In other words, he applies the laws of things and doesn't try to apply the laws of men. If, however, he makes the mistake of handling the men who make the bomber like so much steel and wood, he will have a strike on his hands, instead of bombers.

The nineteenth century was perhaps the greatest century of scientific development the world has ever known, and yet it ended in World War I. Why? Because we developed the laws of things and neglected the laws of men.

Some years ago I heard Kagawa, the famous Japanese Christian, lecture on this subject. He started with the farthest star and concluded with the smallest atom and showed how every unit obeyed the laws of things. Only man has largely ignored the laws of man.

When man traveled at a few miles an hour, the result of this ignorance were not disastrous. A war in one part of the world disturbed others slightly and, except in a few exceptional cases, burned itself out, affecting comparatively small numbers. Today all this is changed. Science has made us all neighbors—physically, if not in spirit. We could hear Hitler while he was speaking. We can have breakfast in America and dinner in London. The art of living together in peace and harmony has become a must. The laws of men must take precedence over the laws of things.

When Steinmetz, the wizard of electricity, was asked what he thought would be the greatest discovery of the future, he instantly replied, "In the realm of the moral, social, and spiritual, we have developed outer laws; we must now develop the inner."

This is an attempt to analyze the more important of these laws as they apply in the lives of everyday people, young and old, at home and in industry. We early discovered that all areas of life must be included if we are to be effective. Life must be brought into focus. We cannot successfully have a Sunday life and a Monday life.

The facts presented are as old as time itself. Our major objective is to persuade people to take action that will result in growth. It is emotion that moves people to doing. We have not learned the value of intelligent emotion. In this article the emphasis is not on the words but in the spirit which we hope to convey. Man is a spirit, not a thing. Briefly, this is not an essay of words.

We have at least seven objectives:

1. This is the only road to the utmost in individual effectiveness and happiness.

2. Here is the only foundation for industrial harmony and teamwork.

3. In these principles the teacher will discover how to kindle the divine flame that leads to great achievement.

4. Here we find the foundation for health through happy, intelligent, effective thinking and living.

5. In such a program, the Church will find new life and become a radiant center for dynamic living.

6. Only thus can we achieve honest national unity.

7. Last, but far from least, the only alternative is a return to the dark ages through a progressive destruction of the values of civilization. We can banish war from the earth in ten years if we are willing to honestly consecrate ourselves to this "way of life."

At first thought you may say that the task is too immense. We can't bring these ideas to 130,000,000 people soon enough. Why not? We have the radio!

Furthermore, the greatest achievements of history have been made possible through small groups. It was Samuel Adams who pointed out the vague yearnings of the colonies toward independence. Patrick Henry crystallized them. George Washington gave them strength and character. At the most, ten men brought about this great turning point in history. It is interesting to note that Adams was "an eminently successful manager of men." "He is considered to have done more than any other one man in the years immediately preceding the war to mold and direct public opinion."

America today is too large for any one man to dominate or direct, but if each one of us is faithful in his small area, this job can be done.

Three hundred men brought about the Renaissance. A handful helped Hitler to gain control of the thinking of a great nation. It is high time we had a great ground swell of democracy that will push these blights from the face of the earth forever—a veritable avalanche of flaming good will, understanding, decency, intelligent unselfishness, and common sense. We must begin now! It is already late. The game is in the last quarter. There are only a few minutes left to play, but it can still be won, if you and I do our part and do not wait around for the other fellow.

If one pursues a program of this sort to its ultimate conclusion, we finally come face to face with the realization that Christ laid down the laws for man in the most perfect form, and that it is only through him that the higher stages of spiritual development can be reached. Many simple character defects can be remedied by human effort. It has been our experience, however, that deep-seated difficulties can be corrected only through a power higher than ourselves. In one case after another we have seen irritable, frustrated, tense personalities achieve poise, balance, and radiance through a combination of earnest effort, love, and faith. In the final analysis it is only as we forget ourselves in something vastly bigger than ourselves that it is possible to achieve balance in personality and character. We must learn to live day by day so intimately in his presence that resentment, fear, and defeat become impossibilities.

The clouds besetting civilization are so thick that human effort alone cannot find a solution. With God all things are possible, but God can only work through you or me. We must become the channels for his love and power and understanding. The world is looking to America for this leadership and we must not fail.

Patterns of Christian Life in Business

MERRICK JACKSON

MEN CAN HARDLY ARGUE over the need for applying Christian principles in daily association.
The consideration of methods for attaining it, however, brings no ready agreement. The way is long
and oftimes uncertain.

On the one hand is a large number of men and
women who desire to Christianize human relations.
On the other is the urgent demand for doing it.
Only the coupling has become complicated.

To obtain thoughtful insight into the problem of
linking this supply and demand, a group of representative laymen were asked to express their points
of view and offer suggestions. Their replies produced
a variety of reactions from confusion to conviction.
They did agree on one point—namely, that the
application of Christian principles, like charity,
begins at home.

One man felt that too many of us talk a good Christian life but rarely put it into action. "There is
plenty of machinery, as well as systems, rules, and
techniques for dealing with these (human relations)
problems," he declared. "But one after another they
go pop over just one snag—the human personality.
By and large—and this always includes me in the

front row—we are a lot of lip-servers. We dabble and
get wordy, but when you peel off the words one by
one you have a neat pile of words and scarcely any
core."

Asked how to convert words to action, he said:
"Why has Jesus left so deep a scratch on the hard surface of the human mind? Surely not for any physical
contribution he made to life. All he seems to have
done is think closer to the line than most and live
according to his thoughts." He might have added
that Christ also knew how to communicate his beliefs
so well that others carried his message far and wide.

Simply living according to one's belief has not
brought satisfaction of attainment to another of the
laymen questioned. The personal experience he
described has doubtless been shared by other sincere
men and women.

"I am definitely a small fry in my organization,"
he explained. "That organization is a family affair in
which all the top executives are a hierarchy, admitting of no encroachment on their prerogatives.
Moreover, most of them are advanced in age, with
fixed habits of Prussian discipline. God knows they
need Christianizing, but I fear little change can be
expected in this generation."

This man tries to be civil, co-operative, uncom-
plaining, and pleasant, but he concludes that "this
is not quite enough." He wonders how he can project a philosophy of right living and thinking to
those about him.

At least a partial answer to his problem is supplied
by a third layman, who stated: "By so living our

daily lives that those with whom we are associated recognize that there is a power behind us reaching out and through us." This man has developed a formula for living that deserves careful scrutiny. It is in three parts:

1. Treat others as we ourselves would like to be treated.

2. Conduct our own individual life so that it serves as a living and outstanding example of the teachings of the Great Teacher.

3. Emulate in our contact with the problems, the frailties, and the shortcomings of others the same type of tolerance and understanding which Christ revealed.

"We all believe that we are individuals with ideals, ideas, and philosophies," he said. "We all desire an opportunity to express ourselves, to the end that we may be not merely cogs in a machine, but individuals in a society. . . . In the last analysis what this means is, of course, viewing daily life from the other person's point of view."

He pointed out that tolerance and understanding do not mean "a sloppy sentimentality in regard to human shortcomings." He went on to say that "Christ was righteously indignant and gave vent to his anger when he drove the money changers out of the temple. There are times and there are circumstances which call for an adamant and unswerving stand or determination."

For those who ponder the perplexities of applied Christianity, this individual offers clear and provocative counsel: "If one wishes truly to affect in a permanent and continuing way the life of another, it can be done by daily continuation of a course of conduct. Precept without example may furnish to others the material which, parrotlike, they may repeat, never understand, and never translate into conduct. Example, on the other hand, is something which permeates, transmutes, and eventually exalts."

To this man, and indeed to many others, one of the most stirring cases of Christianity by example occurred when the cargo transport *Dorchester* was torpedoed ninety miles from Greenland on February 3, 1943. Four chaplains—two Protestant, one Catholic and one Jewish—worked feverishly among the men on the doomed ship. They gave a hand where it was needed, passed out life belts, and murmured words of encouragement to those around them. When more life belts were needed, the chaplains took off their own and passed them over to crew members. As the *Dorchester* sank, men afloat in the icy waters saw the four chaplains standing together, arm in arm in prayer.

Many businessmen, according to one whose views were invited, often find themselves entangled on a dilemma with one horn the profit motive and the other a genuine Christian regard for the other fellow.

"As society is now organized, our whole system of production and distribution would break down if individuals were to disregard material incentives," he said. "In the same way our lives would become disordered if we tried to deny the basic demands of the body, such as hunger and thirst. But just as bodily satisfaction is not an adequate end for living, neither is the accumulation of wealth. Something more is required; some larger goal is necessary. And so I conclude that my aim in business should be to contribute my share of economic production and, at the same time, in every thought and act to draw closer in line to God and man."

Believing that "no amount of money can be worth as much to me as an increased capacity for understanding and loving the people with whom I work," this layman has developed what he calls "spiritual exercises." Here they are:

1. I try in morning prayer and whenever opportunity permits to fix firmly these Christian attitudes of mine.

2. I resolve that I will avoid all forms of egotism and keep myself open and sensitive to each person with whom I come in contact, that I will make every effort to understand him, to discern his needs, and to look for those qualities in him which are admirable and lovable.

3. While I am at work, I try, before making decisions, to hold them up first for God's judgment.

4. When I am tempted to irritation, to greed, to pride, to indulgence in the satisfaction of domination and authority, I attempt to avoid the temptation by a specific internal act of surrendering my will to God.

5. In intercessory prayer in the evening I include in my "prayer list" men and women whom I contact in business.

The suggested program of another layman closely paralleled this in the same important realm of employee relations. He would "pay employees a wage

commensurate with their productive effort even if it
comes out of your own income." He would always
lend a sympathetic ear to employees' personal problems, provide reasonable working hours and assign-
ments, treat workers as though they were members of
his own family, mediate disputes by bringing the
"warring" parties together and invite suggestions for
improved and more harmonious working relationships.

The field of human relations and the application
of Christian principles is so vast and so freighted
with problems requiring specific care that no cure-all
in a thousand words or even ten thousand can be
formulated. Yet, in the viewpoints expressed here,
are both guidance and stimulation.

In the guidance column are these: there are ways
of applying Christian principles. They start with
one's self. Progress toward the goal is in direct ratio
to the faith, determination, and courage of the individual. As he conditions himself to his task, he
recognizes an invisible partnership with a Power
greater than himself. From that partnership he derives increased strength and widening influence. He
no longer stands alone.

There is stimulation in the fact that men are developing patterns of Christian life which are affecting
those around them; that even those men who are
confused or discouraged believe there is a pattern
which they can and must find.

"What the world craves today," said one man in-
terviewed, "is more real Christianity and less formal
religion. It is tired of creeds, sects, rules, dogmas

and precepts but eager for a vital daily relationship with a living God."

Never has there been a greater or more challenging opportunity to help shape a true brotherhood of man. Never has the impelling need for action come more forcibly to the hearts of men. For men of Christian vision and faith, this is the great hour.

Practice of Christian Principles

J. C. PENNEY

WE SHOULD RECOGNIZE OUR TIMES for what they are: periods of tribulation, but not of pessimism. They should inspire us to re-examine our faith and to re-establish our convictions more firmly. As long as we have any faith at all in God, we must know that he is all-powerful, that justice and right are his will for the world, and that eventually his purpose will be established here on earth. Good emerges slowly, but we must not doubt its final outcome.

And just as with individuals, so as a nation will our fate be determined by our choice of the hard right, instead of the easy wrong. America was founded in prayer, in faith, and in the heroic spirit of sacrifice. Comfortable living in easy-going years tends to soften us, and both our spiritual and our physical muscles become flabby. Times like the present are testing periods. The harder they become, the more determined we should be not to be infected by doubts and fears which bedevil the world.

Some of our thinking and many of our practices will have to be revised now that the atomic bomb has been created. We have not understood, and perhaps cannot now fully understand, the changes which the "Atomic Age" will bring to the people of our nation and the world.

I like to think of God as the great power who is taking every opportunity to push mankind along the road to peace and good will. The atomic bomb is one more effort by the Almighty to move us in the right direction. As one writer has put it, "With the advent of the 'Atomic Age,' scientists begin to speak like prophets and statesmen like preachers."

But to talk about the atomic bomb is not enough. The man in the street must be made to see that our chances for survival depends upon our ability to cooperate. For men like ourselves, this means learning how to practice Christian principles in all of our affairs. Are we prepared to begin this practice, each man in his own field of endeavor?

The present state of the world and of people in it does not shake my faith in the ultimate triumph of freedom and justice, for I was reared by parents whose faith in God and whose belief that right will triumph are too deeply ingrained in me to cause me to doubt. My father was an old-school Baptist minister who preached the better part of his lifetime but earned his living as a farmer.

When I was a boy of twelve, I took a load of watermelons to the county fair. Finding a good spot just outside the fair gate, I proceeded with unusual success in selling my product. Just then my father came by and said, "Jim, go home." I asked for more time, but he insisted. Later he said, "Do you think I will permit you to sell those melons outside the gate when men have paid for concessions to sell them inside?"

Shortly after my father died, I bought a butcher shop, investing the $300 I had saved working as a clerk in a dry-goods store. A few weeks later, the butcher told me one morning that if I was to keep the business of the leading hotel in town, I would have to buy the chef a bottle of whiskey every week. I gave little thought to the matter at that time, so I bought the bottle and gave it to him. Afterward a very strange feeling came over me. What would my father have said? What would my mother have thought? I knew the answer to both questions and acted accordingly.

I lost the butcher shop, but I learned a valuable lesson: never to compromise with what I knew to be wrong. At the most critical times of my life, the memory of my father's faith has buoyed me up.

I should like to emphasize one simple truth which I've learned the past few years, that is, being a Christian is not something a man achieves quickly. It is an experience into which we grow and the further we go the more we find is required of us.

Some years ago a bank did me what I considered an injustice, and I held it against them and felt resentment even when their name was mentioned. I used to walk by one of their branch offices, and the very sight of the name brought a feeling of ill-will. Finally, one day not long ago, wanting to get rid of this barrier, I spoke to the doorman as I walked by and, to my surprise, that feeling I had carried so long was removed.

Something has happened in my life the past few years which I find difficult to explain. There has been an inner emptiness which success in business in the usual sense has not satisfied.

It can be partially explained by a new sense in

which I have come to feel the Divine Presence in my life. I am now convinced that the kind of faith men need in God does not come by casual acceptance of a certain standard of moral conduct, important as this is. Rather, men must learn to pray, to remember God all through the day and look to him for inspiration and guidance. To pray until an affection for God and Christ is as real as the affection we have for our families.

I do not mean to give the impression that I have successfully applied Christian principles to all phases of my life. I feel ashamed that I have not followed Christ's teachings as well as I might. I have not loved God as I should. I neglected my obligations to the Church until recent years. I certainly have not worked for the brotherhood of men outside my business to the degree that should be expected of a good Christian. But I am now trying earnestly to make up for what I failed to do.

In my early days, one could put religion in one compartment of his life, his business relations in another, and gain a measure of success. But it is not true in the same way today. The stepped-up business cycle, a product of the industrial revolution and mass production, makes of Christian principles today a virtual necessity. We should study, therefore, with great earnestness the relation between Christ's two commandments: to love God and to love your neighbor as yourself. With a proper balance of these two great laws worked out in our everyday lives, we may be sure of deep spiritual satisfaction and abundant opportunity to serve our fellow man.

V

The Layman at Work in the World

World Security: A Personal Matter

C. J. CHANDLER

THE CIVILIZATION IN WHICH WE LIVE TODAY is extremely complex, much more so than at any other time in history. As we are most acutely aware, the great shortening of distance resulting from our scientific advancement has tremendously increased our social problems. Regardless of our wishes in the matter, we are made a party to the troubles of mankind on the other side of the world and of the peoples in every community between; for not only are the woes of all the human race thrust upon us, but these are greatly accentuated by the demands which our present world-wide intercourse and communication brings with it. Man's wants and desires are whetted and inflamed by knowledge of other people's material advantages, and today the requirements men make of their economic and social orders are more taxing than ever before. This is true of every people in every corner of the world.

This situation presents us with almost staggering problems, deserving our fullest consideration and effort. None of us can be worthy of our responsibility if we give less than our utmost toward their solving. It is not, however, toward such a solution that these remarks are addressed, but rather to consider a deeper reason for our dissatisfaction; for

167

underneath the state of affairs of our world and our
country, there lies a personal instability in the lives
of individual men that is fundamental, and the solution of the world's problems depends, more than we
like to admit, on the improvement we are personally
able to make in this situation.

Human nature being what it is, we and most of
the rest of the races of men are always looking for
a scapegoat; and when things go wrong, as they always do in some degree, we very humanly look everywhere else before we look at home. If we will be
frank with ourselves we will find that we spend a
great deal of our time dwelling on the wrongdoings
and faults, especially the political, social, and economic shortcomings of everyone other than ourselves; and our conversation in modern America,
especially among businessmen, consists, to a startling
degree, in criticism. To prove this it is suggested
that occasion be taken in a conversation where two
or more business or professional people are present,
to refrain from entering into the discussion and
listen from the sidelines. It will often surprise one.
Discussion and just criticism are valuable, and the
world truly is in a terrible state, but underneath all
this is a situation that no amount of economic and
social rearrangement is going to correct. For man's
inner unrest—it is that which we are considering—is
not going to be made whole, even by world-wide
prosperity or complete social harmony, were such a
solution possible.

Is it not our individual uneasiness that today re-
flects itself in a very troubled world? The writer believes that it is, and, furthermore, that what is really

wrong with the world is what is individually wrong with him. This is said because he most sincerely feels that most of us are going out to tackle this world of catastrophe and suffering—and its situation has always been seen to be desperate when we looked at the whole of it, only now its travail is acutely felt by all of us—most of us, may it be repeated, are going out to tackle the responsibility of life with backgrounds of inner consciousness that are very uneasy. Our personal inner consciousness lacks the depth of resource which alone can give life the real meaning it is intended to have. In fact, it is believed many of us are handicapped by a lack of the very resource it is going to be necessary for us to have in the trouble-ladened years that lie ahead, if life is to be worth the living at all.

This is said in the belief that most of us are trying to find in social relationships and in economic readjustments what can be found only in the heart of individual man. We are somewhat like one who looks for the source of a sound by exploring the slopes of a mountain from which an echo comes, never recognizing the place of its origin. That for which we strive is security, for ourselves and for the world, and unconsciously we look for security in all of our struggle, whether it be personal or social. We seek this will-o'-the-wisp in universal education, in world-wide prosperity, in guarantees of self-government, and we call it by such names as liberty, independence, and very often happiness and peace of mind. It is right that we do so strive, for life gives up its secret only through experience; and only when we have tasted the disappointment and disillusionment of all these things by themselves do we realize that it is in man's heart that peace must first be found, and that only in the hearts of men who have discovered this peace can lasting liberty and social justice be established.

We have, quite naturally, looked for this security outside of ourselves. We have sought it in possessions, both material and social, and have felt that it was to be found in something we could construct or build, such as a personal estate, a world empire, or an international organization to police the world. Only occasionally have individual men realized that the one security that really exists is inner security, and that this must be obtained individually, and not in social or political organizations. In fact, such organizations, if they are to endure, must be but the corporate expression of the inner security of men and women who make them up. The individuals that compose them are not secure because of such organization; the organization is secure because of the individuals.

Further, in fixing our hope for security on the arrangement of the physical world, we have more or less unconsciously accepted the belief that all that really exists in our mortal selves. It is true that our religions have told us that we are more than mind and body, and we have often given lip service to such belief, but all the while, for many of us, the attention has remained on the building of our material security structures. This attitude automatically shuts off from us the only avenue by which we may ever hope consciously to fashion security, for we are looking outside ourselves for that which can be found only within. If man is nothing more than mind and body, there is nothing more futile than for him to hope for security for himself or anyone else.

But the real identity of each of us—the real You and real Me—is not just a physical and mental machine; it is a spiritual personality, and could we but realize the truth proclaimed by the founders of all the great religions—that life is not the opposite of death, that death's opposite is really only birth, we would understand that our minds and body are used by our real selves only for the span of years we call life. We then would realize that it is within the depths of our consciousness, and there alone, that security is really to be found.

Such an understanding places the responsibility on each of us, and here we come to that nemesis for most of us: doing something about ourselves. We can often be persuaded to take vigorous action toward the solving of a problem that lies outside of us, especially if we can have companionship in the fight, but when we face the inevitability of our personal selves as a problem we find it much more difficult to move.

Then there is the matter of taking time for introspection when we hardly have enough for that for which we are responsible now. That most of our lives are full no one can question, but it is also true that in the long run we do take time for those things we really most desire to do. Perhaps here we need to weigh the importance of this matter of inner security against the balance of our life's program. How much is the serenity of our life really worth, and how much time can we afford to give ourselves alone to obtain it? For the way must be alone, not for the sake of being alone but for the sake of being, and the most important business of life for each of us is to pursue "our own true way" toward inner strength. By this it is not meant that we should be unsocial —far from it. Nor will the recognition of this responsibility lessen our devotion to any of the worthy objects of life. In fact, inward vitality is the only guarantee against social impotency and political senility. Only individual inward strength can provide society either strength or security, and it cannot help but make us better citizens. But what is suggested is that such security is very difficult to nurture in the atmosphere in which most of our time is spent. To learn to know oneself requires completest attention, and only when the outside stimulations and distractions have been turned off can we begin to become acquainted with our real selves and cultivate our inner peace. It is said of a wise old schoolmaster that he once sent all the boys of his class to their rooms with these instructions: "Go to your room, close the door, sit down, and then answer these three questions: 'Who am I?' 'What am I?' and, 'What am I going to do about it?'" And here are the words of a Danish author who gives, in a few lines, perhaps all that can be said of the pathway toward finding the stability of which I speak:

The most comprehensive formula for human culture I know given by the old peasant who, on his deathbed, obtained from his son only this one promise: To sit every day for half an hour alone in the best room. The son did this and became a model for the whole district. The father had taken thought for everything, for eternity, soul-deepening, refinement, history.[1]

The burden of these remarks then is that the answer to life in the first instance is a personal one. Not that every effort should not be made toward social and economic betterment, but that such improvement cannot permanently rise above the average of man's individual stability. For the writer, the possibility that this presents is not only sobering but extremely hopeful, because it localizes our responsibility at the point where we have absolute authority and control. We may have little effectiveness in correcting an abuse on the other side of the world or even in our own country, but what we can do with ourselves is limited only to our own willingness and ability. Self-criticism is the kind of criticism most likely to produce results even among others.

What a very great part of our time is lived in the surface existence, and how we avoid facing the inadequacies of our own personal lives, Were we not made for something deeper, and is it not probable that our existence here is for the very purpose of awakening us to the realization of something more? We slip through this world, seeming hardly to touch the real part of life; and yet, when the flow of circumstances brings to our lives some great love or, perchance, some great sorrow, we sense a portion of

---

[1] Larsen J. Anker, *With the Door Open,* pp. 100-101. By permission of The Macmillan Company, publishers.

ourselves that is far more tender than we let the
world suspect. Here is the real self that each of us
must find alone, and whose development is the most
important and most personal business of life. Here is
that life in every one of us that lives the truth of our
existence, and in its recognition lies the path to the
only real security we will ever know. May I say more:
in its cultivation rests the one hope of a social structure that can give us lasting peace; for the health of
our social order can only become a reality in a world
of individuals who are consciously strong in themselves.

A modern writer has beautifully retold us a story
of Hans Christian Andersen's in these words:

A nightingale sang so sweetly before the Emperor of China that she was kept in the court and
held in great honor. One day a packet arrived from
another ruler containing the gift of a marvelous
mechanical bird whose songs were an almost perfect imitation of the songs of the living nightingale.
At the first performance of this marvelous rival
the real nightingale flew away. But no one cared,
because, as the music master said, 'With a real
nightingale we can never tell what is going to be
sung, but with this bird everything is settled. We
can open it, and explain it so that people can
understand exactly how the songs are made, why
one particular note follows another.' Finally, when
everyone knew every little turn in the artificial
bird's song, a spring cracked, and the music
stopped. The bird was worn out, and no one
could mend it. Years passed, and the emperor fell

ill. He saw the horrible image of Death bending over him, and he pleaded with the mechanical bird to charm the specter away, but the bird remained silent. Suddenly there came through the open window the sound of a sweet song. Outside on the bough of a tree sat the living nightingale. She sang of the quiet churchyard so beautifully that Death longed to go and see his garden. He floated away like a mist. The emperor recovered, but the living nightingale would come to court no more. She said, "I will sit on a bough outside your window and sing for you, for I love your heart better than your crown."

Only when we realize that no amount of mechanical and social arranging by itself can give us the human order that we so much desire, and learn that security and freedom must first be a song in the heart of individual men and women, will the specter of continual unrest cease to hover over our world.

The Christian Economy

Arthur A. Hood

THE HUMAN RACE has made tremendous progress in recent centuries in understanding God's laws regarding material things, but in the realm of business relations man's understanding and application of God's laws has made little progress.

Two thousand years ago Christ suggested certain new and advanced practices which might deliver us, even today, from the economic evils he specifically condemned. The central theme of this advanced teaching is that physical and material satisfactions are only a part of life.

But every privilege must be maintained by exercise of the duty inherent in the privilege. Every authority used must be matched by an acceptance of equivalent responsibility. The greater the authority, the greater the need for a fearless search for the truth and its acceptance, let the chips fall where they may in the Christian economy.

What kind of a profit can a Christian make and still be a Christian? There seem to be three elements to such profits: first, they should be based on the service performed and equivalent to the value of the service; second, both participants in the transaction should profit by the trade, whether the Christian be the buyer or the seller; third, the profit should be such that were the situation reversed the Christian would consider it a fair deal.

Christ did not hate power; he hated the use of power to the disadvantage of the "little fellow." Under today's economy, the "little man's" skill is his property, the same as the free land he tilled or the waters he fished in Christ's time. In trading his services for other property and in contractual relationships with others, the Christian worker should make the Golden Rule the test of his action.

Mass production—the abundant life in material terms—is here. But we cannot have it or keep it until we learn mass distribution under the principles of the Golden Rule. Distribution involves the application of spiritual meaning to production.

If all the professing Christians among the industrial leadership in America, whether capital, labor or management, would, beginning tomorrow, simultaneously apply the economic teachings of their religion to their own company affairs, the entire industrial life of America would be lifted to the plane of mutual good will and economic peace, instead of bitter dissension, strife, and war; and with it would come higher net profits for all engaged in industry. That is the practicality of idealism.

How can we speed up the know-how of Christian economics? The first step is to take religion out of the Sunday closet and make it a workday tool for living. Christ gave materialism a religious reality. We must give religion economic reality. This means a more extensive search for the truth. Our factual knowledge of how to do right is not equal to our intuitive desire to do right.

Next we laymen can initiate an organized movement to eliminate hate in American life. A change
in employer-employee attitude from an antagonistic
"enemy camps" attitude to a friendly partnership
attitude would dissolve differences that now seem
insurmountable.

This is economic missionary work. In the past,
Christianity has had its evangelical, its educational,
and its medical missionaries, all of whom have
brought important benefits to the convert. An addi-
tional missionary effort might be economic—a practical application of religion to the convert's economic
well-being, giving the basis of a new life in which
God, his neighbor, and the Golden Rule are realities.

The undeniable sterility of religion in economic,
and political life must end. It is not Christianity
that is sterile; it is we Christians.

A New Scale of Values

CHERRY L. EMERSON

"YOU SHALL KNOW THE TRUTH and the truth shall make you free."

The question asked by Pontius Pilate, "What is truth?" still echoes down the ages.

Indeed, there are many aspects of truth. One of these is the truth about the laws of nature and our physical environment. These are the truths with which science has dealt, always with increasing success, and particularly in the last three generations.

The two greatest forces in the world today, and those on which the immediate future of civilization rests, are religion and science. In the past, certain people have felt that these great forces might be opposed to each other, that we could not believe both the revealed truth of religion and the experimental truth of science. Today we know that they are not opposed, but complement each other. Tomorrow they should go forward hand in hand, rendering mutual aid and comfort. That they should do so is a matter of life or death.

The misunderstanding has probably arisen in this way. Some thoughtless people who have been benefited by the advance of the healing art, or who have realized the power and productivity of the machine age, have been carried away with the physical evi-

dence of material progress. They have rushed to a
conclusion of their own that all problems can be
solved by medical or mechanical means; that all the
needs of men can be met by more physical and biological science. Worse, they have concluded that the
universe is a great machine and men are controlled
like machines.

The scientists themselves are not, however, num-
bered among these thoughtless ones. Their leaders,
for a long time, have realized that science does not
point the way to a philosophy of mechanism or re-
strict the operation of free will. Certainly, recent discoveries lead to a very different conclusion. Among
a great number of other facts is the electrical com-
position of matter, that all material things are com-
posed of atoms and these in turn of nothing but par-
ticles of electricity revolving like a solar system. The
only satisfactory definition of electricity is that it is
energy; so men of learning have explained matter by
explaining it completely away.

Thus we have a strange paradox, that while we
have the uninformed quoting science as teaching
materialism, the real scientists themselves say that
the universe is not like a great machine, but more
like a great thought.

Our Saviour has said that he came "so that men
might have life and that they might have it more
abundantly." For two thousand years, the Church
has carried on his work to this end, and recently science has also made its contribution. We say *recently*
in the scale of recorded history, which runs back
some five thousand years. The beginnings of modern

science were with Galileo about three hundred years
ago; it came into flower during the life of Isaac New-
ton about two hundred years ago; and it was almost
exactly one hundred years ago, in 1840, that Faraday
and Maxwell laid down the experimental foundation
in the laws of electricity and magnetism from which
has sprung our great cordon of electrical transmission,
knitting our industrial system together with a web of
power. Man has made more progress in the effort to
control his environment during the last one hundred, or even the last fifty years, than in all of the
other forty-nine hundred years of recorded time.

The achievements of the last one hundred years,
made possible by science, have done much more than
give us a bewildering series of new gadgets and machines. They have done more than make us unbe-
lievably comfortable as contrasted with the conditions of my own youth.

We may think of the wonders wrought by the
medical profession in saving the lives of children,
in relieving pain, in lengthening the span of life; but
these fields are outside of my experience. The physical sciences alone have contributed so much it
would take hours to catalogue them. Consider for a
moment that we have the news of the whole world
of the previous day laid at our breakfast table in the
form of a newspaper; that a person, whether mounte-
bank, commentator, or prophet, may speak to the
entire world by radio; that in the past years we have
been able by automobile to visit every nook and
cranny of our country and find friends among people
we might have otherwise considered as enemies.

More than all this, we have been given the priceless gift of leisure which some day we may learn to rightly use.

Yes, man has conquered his environment and that conquest can soon be made absolute. Yet he has not conquered himself. Here we encounter the limitation of science, and it is a limitation which may in somber fact be fatal. Science has no scale of values. It deals with the question, "true or untrue?" It does not ask the question, "good or bad?" What man shall do with the new opportunities of control which science has given him does not depend upon science but upon what man wants to do with them and this in turn depends upon his scale of values.

As Sir James Jeans said, "Science fishes in the sea of reality with a particular kind of net called the scientific method, and there may be much in the unfathomable sea which the meshes of science cannot catch." This means that science in its own sphere of knowledge is supreme; in other spheres it is only a method or a tool.

The vital importance of these two aspects of science—its tremendous power and its fatal limitation—has been brought home to us. All the great knowledge and energies of all the scientists and scientific institutions, not only in this country but of the whole world, were diverted from their normal pursuits and focused on the ghastly business of destruction. Who can compress in a sentence or two the tragedy of millions of deaths and wounds, or all the pain, anguish, fear, and holocaust of war? Will blind science, without a scale of values, pull down the pillars of the temple of civilization?

Looking to the future, we realize that unless civilization is literally to destroy itself, we must have this scale of values which science is powerless to supply. It can come only from religion. I do not mean from forms or creeds, but from deep within the spirit of man. Perhaps the harrowing our souls have received from war was the necessary preparation of the soil.

Jesus Christ has given us a perfect scale of values. It was revealed to him by the Omnipotent Spirit of Truth of whom Jesus said, "Thy word is truth." This scale is all contained in the first four books of the New Testament. All the rest is commentary. These can be read thoughtfully in four days. In them is the sole hope of the world.

Most of us say to ourselves that the words of these books are not meant literally and that the teachings are impractical. The scale of values is too high; we would have to sacrifice too much if we followed them literally. Perhaps the time is near when we may have the choice of trying to follow them literally or else live continuously with war preparation our sole business, and eventual war our sole expectation.

Perhaps not science but the scientific method has some slight help to offer. Its method is that of experiment. It is always and forever trying; a hundred failures do not discourage the scientist from the one hundred and first attempt. So many of us come to service on Sunday and are emotionally stirred, but during the next six days do not try as we should to put in practice the truths which we have learned. We might at least experiment prayerfully to apply our scale of values. Perhaps we could study such small successes as others have been able to make.

Laymen Speaking

Certainly our small beginnings, no matter how feeble, will not be dismissed as negligible by the Omnipotent Spirit of Truth.

Religion and science are continually being drawn together by a great necessity. If religion will make its scale of values active in the lives of its followers, they can use the powers of science to build here and now that kingdom of which Jesus so often spoke, and thus remake the world for peace.

Trends in America Which Affect Our Economic Life

Thomas J. Watson

At no time in the history of civilization have laymen been so badly needed to assist our spiritual and education leaders who are giving their lives to the development of our young people.

The world we leave our children depends on a number of things. Most important are the parents of the children. What kind of teaching must we give our children? And, more important than what we teach, what kind of example are we setting for our children?

We laymen are setting an example. If we were to go before any audience tonight and ask, "How many of you people would like to have all the churches eliminated from our various communities?" we know we would not get very many votes. Everyone would say, "I think the churches are a good thing and I would not want to see them removed from the community."

The next thought is, what are we doing in support of the Church? I do not mean financial support. That is the least. What are we doing in the way of example for the children we are talking about in the future world? Are we setting an example by going to church and backing up the minister?

The opportunities that we are going to leave our children are tremendous. Just compare these opportunities with those we had when we started. Think of the many new things that have come into being during our lives. Think of the natural resources that have been developed, the foreign trade that has been built up, and the greater access to raw materials from all the different countries in the world. Before we went to war the United States was manufacturing 47 per cent of everything manufactured in the world, and consuming more than 90 per cent of it right here at home.

Let us compare the tools our children are going to have with the tools we had to work with. Let us point out to them that they stand on the threshold of a new era with all these new things at their command, and that they must do a better job than their fathers did; that they must carry on for the benefit not only of the United States but of the world.

The war brought the United States to a point in our civilization where it must assume the responsibility for world leadership. The most important work in which we must assume leadership is developing the laymen of the country into a great force for good.

We can be successful in this because we have faith. We have faith in our Maker, in our country, in our world, and in ourselves. Our faith enables us to do something worthwhile.

Let us always keep in mind what was done by twelve men, limited in education and limited in resources, but with an abundance of faith in divine leadership. They established Christianity, the greatest thing that has ever come to the world, and it has grown stronger and stronger throughout the ages. Nothing shattered the faith of those men.

In speaking of our children's opportunities, I wonder how often we give consideration to what the improvements in our methods of communication mean to us and to our everyday life. In our press, motion pictures, radio, and other means of communication we have the greatest educational institutions in our land.

We are constantly increasing the number of those who go to college. We can be very proud that there are 1,500,000 in our institutions of higher learning. Yet, although 26,000,000 start in primary schools, only 7,200,000 ever get to high school, and of these only half have an opportunity to go through, while only 1,500,000 go into colleges and universities. Still, we can boast a little about the latter figure because we have more students in institutions of higher learning than the rest of the world combined.

In addition to colleges, consider the fine articles written by the most intelligent men and women in the country and published in our newspapers and magazines, the fine talks that are broadcast by radio, and the fine books that are written on every subject. Let us see what we as laymen can do toward getting our children to realize what good reading and listening to good speakers can do. Many children are going to be handicapped by inability to get as much formal education as they want, and we can point out this way for them to supplement what education they start with, as many of us have done.

There is today, and has been for some time, a

great deal of talk about atomic power. I heard a
lady say the other night that she wished it never had
been heard of. But it would be a sad thing for us
here tonight if it had not been developed. We have
been through seven major wars since we became an
independent country and still we think we are a
country at peace. That is an average of a war every
twenty-seven years, and in every case, in order to
win, we had to develop greater power for destruction
than our enemies. That is what we did this time.

What have we done with these powers for destruction that we developed during the other wars? We
have always put them to good use in peacetime, and
that is what we are going to do with atomic power.

There is talk about atomic power destroying mankind. It never is going to be used for that. God did
not create the universe, bring it to this point, and
then wish to destroy everybody. We have had means
for doing that for years and years, and in a much
less expensive way. It could have been done through
the spreading of disease. It could have been done
through the use of poison gas, developed during the
First World War. Atomic power today has a place
in our country and in our world, and everybody
knows that we are never going to use it for destruction.

The two greatest powers that have come to the
world have never been fully developed. These are
spiritual power and educational power; and, as laymen, I think if we will do a better job in the development of those two powers, they will guide us
in the proper use of all other powers. No power has

ever made other powers obsolete. It has only supplemented them.

What does it all boil down to? Man power! After all these powers were discovered and developed they were absolutely useless until men made use of them. Our job is the simple one of teaching more people to make better use of spiritual and educational power, for through them we can learn how to handle all other powers.

Christianity Is Practical

John J. Porter

Jesus is the most practical man who ever lived. Not only is Christianity practical, but it is the only way of saving this world from its troubles and giving us as individuals the one thing we all want.

Christianity is practical as applied to international, political, and social problems. Mankind is in a bad way. We are sitting on a powder keg and living on borrowed time. Our trouble is that we have been too smart in building a Frankenstein of material progress, but not wise in that we have failed to provide spiritual controls for this monster. Without such controls, science, invention, mass production, and atomic energy bring to the human race, not happiness, but only more disputes and dangers.

Many people are saying that the Church has proved its impotence, that Christianity has failed. Karl Marx once said that he would found his movement on a more dynamic force, namely, class antagonism, instead of human brotherhood, which had been tried for eighteen centuries and failed.

But have the teachings of Jesus failed? Is it not true that "No nation has ever yet given Jesus a chance to show what he could do for a people wholly living up to his teachings"? Great minds have long recognized that the only way out of our human mess is through the principles of Christianity. Nearly two hundred years ago Benjamin Franklin said, "He who shall introduce into public affairs the principles of primitive Christianity will change the face of the world." Recently General MacArthur has stated that "The problem is basically theological. . . . It must be of the spirit if we are to save the flesh."

This generation has learned through sad experience what former generations have proved over and over again: that the use of force leads only to bigger and better wars. To achieve peace, industrial, social, or national, we must fall back on the methods taught by Jesus in his Sermon on the Mount. When used they have never failed.

Christianity is also practical because it is the only sure way of giving us as individuals the one thing we all want, namely, true happiness. Most of us try to get it in other ways, through money, power, amusements, or forgetfulness induced by drugs, such as alcohol or opium. Experience proves, however, that none of these things alone is adequate, for the very good reason that happiness comes from within; it is a spiritual and not a material possession and it involves that inner life referred to by Jesus as the Kingdom of Heaven.

Obstacles to happiness all center in self. Fear, worry, disappointments, hurt feelings, jealousy, anger, all come to us through thoughts of self. Jesus teaches that we should subordinate self and put God first, loving him with all our heart and with all our soul and with all our mind. If we do this we will be poor in spirit—that is, humble—and we will be blessed by finding the Kingdom of Heaven, that pearl of great price, more valuable than all other possessions.

Again, Christianity is practical, because this Kingdom of Heaven that we may possess through the teachings of Christ is the only possession that we can take with us into eternity.

Hendrik Van Loon opens his *Story of Mankind* with this legend: "High up in the North in the land called Svithjod, there stands a rock. It is a hundred miles high and a hundred miles wide. Once every thousand years a little bird comes to this rock to sharpen its beak. When the rock has thus been worn away, then a single day of eternity will have gone by."

Which, then, is the more important, life or eternity? And how foolish it is for us to spend so much of our thought and effort on the material things which are here today and gone to morrow, and so little on the spiritual things, the really practical things, which last forever.

> The glories of our blood and state
> Are shadows, not substantial things.
> There is no armor against fate,
> Death sets his icy hand on kings.
> > Scepter and Crown
> > Must tumble down,
> And in the dust be equal made
> With the poor crooked scythe and spade.

Still again Christianity is practical because through it we can tap a source of power that will not only prepare us for the life to come, but will also help us in the affairs of this life.

This phase of Christianity is too often overlooked.

God is our heavenly Father, and he wants to give us all the good things that are good for us to have. The teachings of Jesus are good economics and good business and if we follow them we are likely to meet with more success in our material undertakings than would otherwise be the case.

This is well illustrated by a story of John Wesley. As you know, his ministry was to the desperately poor in the slums of England's cities. After a few years, however, his converts showed indications of prosperity. They had stopped drinking and gambling, worked regularly, saved their earnings, and many of them had acquired small but prosperous businesses. Wesley, when he realized the change, and having in mind the dangers of wealth, made this classic remark: "The Methodist Church is becoming prosperous. Something will have to be done about it."

However, the help we can have goes far beyond this. God not only offers us very powerful, potent, and practical aids, but he came to this earth himself in the person of Jesus, to explain to us how to use them. I refer to the power of prayer when coupled with faith and implemented by work. Prayer, Faith, Work: this constitutes a formula for success.

I am aware that many people regard prayer as a form of superstition, and that many Christians consider it only a formality of no particular importance. However, Jesus laid great stress on it and said that, "Whatsoever ye ask in prayer believing, ye shall receive," and the evidence of the validity of this promise is overwhelming.

Dr. Alexis Carrel, research scientist at the Rocke-

feller Institute, Nobel prize winner and author of
the book *Man the Unknown,* makes these statements
on the basis of his biological researches: "Prayer is
the most powerful form of energy that one can gen-
erate." "The influence of prayer on the human
body is as demonstrable as that of secreting glands."
"Prayer, like radium, is a source of luminous, self-
generating energy."

Examples without number of this power could be
given. I have had personal experiences which leave
me no room for doubt and the same must be true
with most of us. However, if there are any doubters,
I urge they get and read Dr. Frank Laubach's book,
Prayer, the Mightiest Force in the World. The examples there given of the power of prayer, and the
explanations of its techniques and use make this, in
my opinion, one of the most valuable and practical
books ever published.

Now we must admit that there are some cases in
which prayers are apparently unanswered, and considering our lack of wisdom and frequently foolish
requests, it is evident that if God did indiscriminately
grant all petitions, we individuals and the world as
a whole would probably be worse off than now. This,
no doubt, is the reason why Jesus is so insistent that
we include in all our prayers the phrase: "Nevertheless thy will be done."

Other reasons why some prayers are seemingly not
answered may be as follows: An all-wise God cannot,
in our best interest, answer all prayers, Yes. To many
of them he must say, No, and to still others, Wait.
Too many of us are like the small boy who said that
some nights he skipped his prayers because he could

not think of anything he wanted. Purely selfish prayers for things that very likely would do us harm are not apt to be answered.

There is a story of a preacher who came across a driver of a stalled truck. Shocked at the profanity, he suggested prayer instead. The truck driver, willing to try anything once, said a prayer, then stepped of his starter and, lo and behold, the truck started, leaving the preacher startled and staring and repeating, "Well I declare; it did work, didn't it?" This illustrates the fact that too many of us fail to pray "believing," and our lack of faith often stands in the way of results.

However, our most common fault is our failure even to attempt to lay hold on this power that God offers us. As Benjamin Franklin put it, "In this situation of this assembly, groping as it were in the dark to find political truth, and scarcely able to distinguish it when presented to us, how has it happened that we have not hitherto once thought of humbly applying to the Father of all light to illuminate our understanding?"

A young man once came to his minister with a long complaint of the injustice, the wickedness, and the hopelessness of the world. He wound up with a complaint against God for creating such a world and the statement that, "I could make a better world myself." To which his minister, being a wise man, replied, "That's just exactly what God wants you to do."

The practical man says "results are what count," and God, being practical, wants us Christian laymen to produce practical results in bringing his Kingdom to this world. We all have our work to do. Some have the responsibilities of leadership, some are technical experts, but most of us are just privates in the ranks and can only contribute our mite in our own small field of activity.

But if we feel discouraged at our seeming impotence, let us remember that there is one very practical thing that everyone can do—that is, pray, and through prayer lay hold on the infinite power of God and focus it on the problems of individuals and of the world.

And let us remember that "It is better to light a candle than to curse the darkness."

The God We Seek

C. Alexander Capron

THE TRAGEDIES OF THE WAR AND THE PEACE are beginning to make their impression upon us all. In spite of sacrifices, men are still self-seeking, greedy, lustful, and filled with envy, hatred, and malice.

We cannot help asking why this is so. The failure is not God's. He has revealed to us how we may live in peace and happiness. We have listened and gone our own way. We have not really tried Christianity as a practical way of life. How long shall we be blind to our opportunities?

Dr. Glenn Clark continually emphasizes the phrase earlier used by Brother Lawrence: "the practice of the presence of God." In the face of uncertainty in our lives today this way to find our peace should provoke a ready response, and become for us a common experience, not merely in church but in our homes and in our offices. We may gain this experience if we want to. If we relax our hold on personal desires, ambitions, self-interests, and ask God to let us know his will, we may become conscious of his presence. If we fear to know his will we shall not find him. We must be willing to learn what he would have us do.

When we seek the presence of God, let us remem-

ber that he is the God revealed by Jesus Christ. What
do we know of him?

Before Jesus started his ministry, he withdrew
from the world in which he had lived to learn his
Father's will, and throughout his ministry he withdrew from those about him to commune with God.
The results of that communion are shown in his
ministry.

Kagawa and Gibran, two Easterners who probably
have more understanding than we of the environment in which Jesus lived, find in the gospels the
portrait of a happy and joyful man. But Jesus was
much more than that. He was a man of action. He
was untiring in his service to others. He was a man
of strength and power. He had power over men's
minds as well as their bodies. While his disciples
marveled at his power, having discerned that power,
they were not astonished at his seeming inexhaustible
strength to carry on his ministry. So great was his
power that his work was apparently effortless. We
find nothing to suggest that Jesus was ever overwhelmed by stress or strain.

Not only power and strength, but happiness and
serenity and peace pervaded him and flowed from
him. But his serenity was not the tranquillity of
contemplation like that of the Hindus. His was the
serenity of strength and power in action.

The God we seek, then, requires positive action
on our part, service to others. If with confidence we
seek to know what he would have us do, we will find
the strength and power to accomplish his purpose for
us. As we go forward, we will also find the joy of

living and doing, and we may be certain that the confidence and serenity that pervaded Jesus will be found only in active service.

Jesus also revealed that the God we seek is a Father of infinite love. He is not only our Father but the God and Father of all men. Therefore, we are united to all men and must be mindful of them wherever they may be.

Anything that we may do to ease men's burdens and to make them strong in mind and body and spirit and bring them happiness is within the scope of the service which Jesus rendered. There is one supreme task, however, and that is to reveal God to others. This must be done by telling them of him and by our actions. Only by doing for others may we reveal God to them, as Christ revealed him to us. This task must continue until God is known to all men.

What will be the fruition? Instead of war, peace; in place of poverty and degradation, prosperity and happiness, a sharing by all in the bounty and beauty of this glorious earth. Surely, when all men live as Jesus lived, seeking the happiness of others, we will realize the Kingdom of Heaven on earth.

And what of those engaged in such a great adventure? We know deep within us that the satisfaction of working creatively is its own reward. Jesus said he came to give us more abundant life.

Some believe that the world we desire may be created by engaging in humanitarian work. We will join them in that work, but that is not enough. Though we may give men more material things, we shall not see the world we desire so long as men are bound by self. Men must be changed. Some will say that we should educate them so that they may know where enlightened self-interest leads. But so long as self-interest occupies the center of the stage, I have no confidence in the result.

There is one sure way. Let us take it. Let us help men to find the God revealed by Jesus Christ.

A Practical View of Labor Relations

JAMES S. CRUTCHFIELD

THE "PRICELESS INGREDIENT" of successful labor relations is a simple principle known to all students of the problem, a principle that may be said to apply equally well to all the difficult social, economic, and political questions with which we are currently concerned, namely, the principle of the Golden Rule. The record indicates rather plainly that the adjustment of conflicting points of view on the part of capital and labor is only possible when both parties approach the task with open minds, with a disposition to seek out the truth, with a will to compromise extreme positions, and with a deep sense of obligation to the public interest. Upon the assumption that the free enterprise system should prevail, a reconciliation of the conflicting views of capital and labor derives principally from the attitude and frame of mind of the parties involved, from their willingness, in language familiar to those who hold firmly to Christian convictions, to relate all finite problems to the basic oneness of human destiny in the sight of God. We deal here with a fundamental matter: when men come together to view their common problems with right motives the major obstacle to a meeting of minds has already been hurdled.

That this principle has been far more honored in theory than in practice is all too evident. It is the common error of some people and of some groups —all of us, perhaps, at one time or another—representing both employer and employee interests to impute all manner of sinister purposes, each to the other. It must be admitted that in some cases the record would seem to justify a good deal of skepticism. Labor has had to fight most of the way to its present position of influence and power, and has good reason for assuming that some of the employer groups are not entirely willing to concede that labor has every right to organize for the purposes of collective bargaining and security; that, indeed, the worker's collective strength is the only means of balancing the power which inheres in the control of our huge industrial establishments. Employers, too, can point to instances of abuse of power on the part of labor leaders and of failures to honor contractual obligations.

The more serious aspect of this matter of questioning motives, and of reading the record so as to support one's own point of view, concerns the manner in which appeals are made to prejudice, in an effort to place the opposing group at a disadvantage before the bar of public opinion.

An interesting example of mistaken opinion was revealed recently by Elmo Roper, public opinion survey expert for *Fortune,* in his syndicated column to newspapers throughout the country. Mr. Roper conducted a spot survey in four of the largest industrial centers in the United States in an effort to measure the extent to which businessmen felt that strikes slowed down production schedules between Pearl Harbor and V-J Day. It was learned that 62.8 per cent felt that production had been slowed down by a month or more as a result of strikes, and 83.5 per cent were convinced that we should have been at least a few weeks ahead had labor indulged in no strikes during the period of the war. The facts in the case, however, as Mr. Roper points out, are considerably at variance with the opinions of most of our businessmen. Actually, all the man-hours lost in strikes between December 7, 1941, and August 14, 1945, totaled less than four days of production time —or about the amount of working time made up by the sacrifice of the four Fourth of July holidays by most of our workers. Amid the present chaos of postwar economic adjustments it is clearly evident that in this vital field of labor-management relations the art of constructive statesmanship is in desperate need of cultivation. A first step on the part of the representatives of both labor and industry could well be the exercising of a large degree of self-criticism and self-restraint.

Emil Schram, president of the New York Stock Exchange, formerly head of the RFC and a Presbyterian layman, said in a recent address:

> During the last decade, under a sympathetic Government, many of the earlier goals of the workers have been recognized as a matter of law, and a widespread appreciation of the human values in industrial relations has developed. Mr. Elmo Roper has made a survey designed to find out what labor really wants. After much processing of answers to a wide variety of questions, it was found that labor principally wanted

four things, the first of which was security—not the
security provided by Government aid, but rather the
right to work regularly at reasonably good wages in
the employ of private industry. The second desire was
for the chance to advance, to go from one job to a
better job. The third was a more intangible desire
and one which has frequently received too little consideration. It is a desire to be treated as a human
being and not as a pay-roll number. The worker wants
the respect of his employer, his fellow workmen, and
his neighbors. The fourth desire could be described
as a social consciousness—a confidence that he is doing
a good job that needs to be done, a feeling that he
plays an essential role.

If the worker's aspirations which I have mentioned
are to be realized under the mass production system,
as they should be, we must use our best leadership,
both in the field of management and in the field of
labor. The question is partly a moral one that calls
for spiritual leadership as well as industrial statesmanship.

I believe that this country has come to accept a
permanent advance in the position of labor in our
social and economic structure.

The public is increasingly impatient with the irresponsibility of certain labor leaders. The public, as
labor will learn and as business has learned, is a hard
taskmaster. Slow to wrath, the public ultimately imposes penalties for irresponsibility.

As we are willing to recognize organized labor and
extend to it rights and privileges under the law, so
must organized labor accept its full stature under the
law and undertake those responsibilities which go
along with rights.

The chief executives of business and labor organizations should get together frequently in a spirit of genuine friendship, with a desire to understand each other's viewpoint and problems, and with the determination to find the right answer to actual or threatened differences.

The prevalence of strikes in this enlightened age is evidence that the lessons of war have not yet been learned by business and labor. This is due in part to the fact that business executives have failed to recognize that the maintenance of good relations with their worker associates is or should be their chief concern. They should take the initiative in improving their relationship with the workers. Workmen, through their powerful unions, have political power far superior to, though not so dramatic as, the strike weapon. Strikes, like war, are self-destructive. In some instances the effect is more harmful to workmen than to business, with the innocent public the chief victim.

The abuse of great power is a calamity to everyone. How to use it constructively is the big problem confronting powerful business and powerful labor organizations. As a nation we have demonstrated great skill in using our might destructively, notably in the development of the atomic bomb. We need to develop skill in using our might constructively for the human good.

There are times, and this period of reconversion from war to peace seems to be one of them, when we seem not to apprehend the nature of the crisis in which we find ourselves. It should be crystal clear to all, following the most horrible war in all history, that our civilization is in deep trouble, and that the manner in which we handle the acute problems abroad and at home during the next five years will indicate whether we are capable of providing an answer of sufficient scope for the crisis at hand.

It is our conviction that the free enterprise system is an essential part of a democratic society, but we must recognize that this view has been discarded by many peoples, including that oldest of living democracies, Great Britain. Our contention in this regard, therefore, is on trial. If we do not create in America, through the free enterprise system, a high degree of employment, a standard of living progressively better for all our citizens, an answer that seems relatively permanent to the vexing problem of the business cycle, and some solution to the problem of relations between capital and labor, then it will be evident, and in not too many years, that experiment along socialistic lines in this country will be unavoidable.

There is an important role that the Church can and ought to play in bringing about better relations between labor and capital, and bringing to bear upon its membership a greater understanding of the nature of such problems. The Church, at its best, is a servant of truth, and a bearer of good news about the abundant life. It is the job of the Church, as such, to prepare men for great social tasks, and to keep constantly before their minds the exceedingly practical teachings of Jesus on the proper manner in which we should conduct our relations, one with another.

No man committed to Jesus Christ and his Golden Rule can stoop to the corrupting of the instruments of public opinion, nor seek self-gain at the expense of the public interest. Nor can he be other than humble as he deals with the usually complicated and frequently explosive nature of human affairs. When a man comes to regard all men, as well as himself, as members of God's family, he may then be said to be ready to contribute something of lasting value.